DAKOTA
at War

Arthur Pearcy

LONDON

IAN ALLAN LTD

First published 1982

ISBN 0 7110 1217 2

Published by Ian Allan Ltd, Shepperton, Surrey; and printed by Ian Allan Printing Ltd at their works at Coombelands in Runnymede, England

Jacket: Painting of Flt Lt David Lord's blazing Dakota over Arnhem on 19 September 1944. For his valour Lord was awarded a posthumous VC. *Reproduced by kind permission of The Air Officer Commanding No 38 Group, RAF, Upavon, Wiltshire.*

Previous page: Two C-47 Skytrains from SCAT with a top cover of Curtiss P-40 fighters, seen somewhere in the South-west Pacific theatre. *Sad Sack* is a C-47-DL 41-18573 c/n 4698 which was finally condemned on 13 January 1943. *US Navy*

Contents

Introduction

12th Air Force Troop Carrier Wing Douglas C-47 Skytrains from the
81st Troop Carrier Squadron, which operated from Middle East bases, are
seen on their way to drop paratroopers during the invasion of
Southern France on 15 August 1944. Aircraft in the photo are 43-15661
U5-X C-47A-90-DL c/n 20127 and 42-100550 U5-F C-47A-65-DL c/n
19013. *USAF*

The transition of the Douglas DC-3 civil transport aircraft into one of the vital strategic weapons of World War 2, marks a crucial chapter in the revolution of military air transport as a whole. The Douglas Commercial series commenced with the one and only DC-1 which first flew on 1 July 1933. The US airlines soon recognised the type as a potential profit maker and in production it became the uprated DC-2 which first flew on 11 May 1934. From then on the aircraft was a success story for both the Douglas Aircraft Company, and its founder and leader, Donald Wills Douglas. This success was further reinforced with the introduction of the ubiquitous DC-3 which was serving the airlines of the world, including those in Europe, in large numbers when World War 2 began in September 1939.

The success of the DC-2s on the internal airways of the USA alerted the US Army Air Corps to the aircraft's potential as a transport for troops and military equipment. The strategic necessity of being able to transfer troops from coast to coast in a matter of hours rather than by rail over days had long been recognised but until the DC-2 arrived adequate means had not existed. Even the miserly US Congress was persuaded to provide funds to buy specimen aircraft for the Air Corps and the first one, a DC-2, was bought in 1936. It was powered by two Curtiss Wright 700hp radial air-cooled engines and weighed 18,200lb gross.

The US Army Air Corps at Wright Field had done static tests with a Douglas DC-2 during 1935, the aircraft finally breaking up under loads three times its design limitations.

Future procurement of Douglas transport aircraft became part of each succeeding budget for the military, and the demand for military cargo aircraft increased. The Tenth Air Transport Group was formed with Douglas C-33 and C-39 transports at Patterson Field, near Dayton, Ohio during 1939. This was the home base of the huge Fairfield Air Depot, one of a whole nationwide system of Supply Depots under the Air Corps Material Division based a few miles down the highway at Wright Field, the test and procurement centre for all Air Corps Operations. The new transport group started their own military airline, linking the Fairfield Air Depot with others located at Middletown, Pennsylvania; Sacramento, California; Portland, Oregon; and Salt Lake City, Utah. The Douglas air freighters of this newly organised transport unit flew daily schedules between the depots. By the end of 1941, the 16-seat Douglas C-39s had further chances to prove themselves. They were called upon to perform many rigorous transport operations in the early days of the US involvement in World War 2. They ferried supplies to Goose Bay, Newfoundland, and flew survivors out of the Philippines to Australia in December 1941.

Additional cargo carrying capacity soon became necessary. But extra pay load meant increased gross weight and additional engine power to maintain a good performance. Douglas converted a C-39 at the factory before completion to C-41 standard by fitting two Pratt & Whitney radial air-cooled engines developing 1,200hp each. This additional engine power raised the speed to 225mph and improved take-off characteristics. Gross weight increased to 26,314lb. Until the procurement of the Douglas C-41, C-41A and C-42, the general configuration of the cargo aircraft was comparable to the airline DC-3, except that on some models cargo doors were installed. On the advent of war other modifications and performance adjustments com-

Right: An 'Oddentification' of the ubiquitous military version of the famous Douglas DC-3 airliner, drawn especially for the author by Chris Wren, originator of the World War 2 series of aeroplane caricatures which ran for five years in the now defunct *Aeroplane* magazine. It is based on his original 26 March 1943, drawing of the type.

patible with military requirements had to be made. On the C-41, C-41A and C-42, the cargo floor of the fuselage was strengthened, tie down rings were made heavier, and the aft fuselage structure strengthened. The cargo doors were also enlarged — and all of these modifications to the basic structure increased the gross weight.

Late in 1939, the planners of the US Army Air Corps drew up the basic specification of an improved Douglas transport to be known as the C-47. The whole concept was based on an aircraft that could be mass-produced for the impending war. The previous experience of the Douglas technicians in the production of military air transports, and the fact that the basic DC-3 lent itself to a good production breakdown both augured well for mass output. However, manufacturing operations would have to be revolutionised. The Army Air Corps outlined to Douglas the changes required — stronger cabin floor, strengthened rear fuselage and large loading doors, more powerful engines and provisions for carrying cargo with supply packs fitted externally. Most of the design work on the military version of the DC-3 had already been completed when the first orders were placed, in 1940, for large numbers.

It is not generally realised that the military version of the DC-3 could well have been rejected when the US entered World War 2. Long successful in civilian passenger service the DC-3 was considered obsolete at the time of Pearl Harbor. It had many features ill suited to the convenient handling of bulky freight, and its payload was too low for the new tasks. But it was flyable under almost all conditions, was easily maintained and, above all, was in production. The DC-3 was a low-wing monoplane whose fuselage stood so high off the ground that loading from an ordinary truck platform was impractical. Also the door was narrow and the floor lacked the strength to support heavy cargo. A larger door, reinforced floor, special loading equipment, and other improvisations were devised for the C-47, but it was natural that US Air Transport Command should have sought an aircraft better suited to its needs. At this stage it was not envisaged just how successful the 'Gooney Bird' would be, despite its shortcomings.

The first Douglas transports to enter Royal Air Force service were the 12 received by 31 Squadron in April 1941 — all Douglas DC-2s. A total of 25 DC-2s was bought by the British Purchasing Commission in Washington, DC, during 1941, the first 15 being earmarked for the Government of India who originally intended their use by Tata Airlines and Indian National Airway. In the event, only the first 12 reached India and they were diverted to the RAF before seeing service with either airline. Three Douglas DC-2s were delivered to 117 Squadron in the Middle East during October 1941, one in November and December, plus one in July 1942. In the RAF inventory they were known as the

DC-2K. It must be remembered that these transports, and the DC-3s that followed, used by the RAF were already veterans. Some of the engines, a mixture of Wright Cyclones and Pratt & Whitney Twin Wasps, already had a history of 10,000 hours, or more, when the RAF took them over. They arrived in the theatre of operations at a time when they were required almost incessantly, and therefore inspections, which were routine elsewhere, had to be skimped. Everything was a matter of improvisation as there were no spare parts for replacements. However, the RAF pilots had great faith and affection for their new transport aircraft.

With the arrival of the DC-3 into the RAF's inventory more pilots were required and some crews from 31 Squadron were trained by US military pilots at Karachi on Santa Monica-built Douglas C-53 Skytrooper transports. The early Douglas types gave valiant service in the Middle East and India, and it was to be another year before the first RAF C-47 Dakota would be available.

In the UK the British Airborne Forces were using aircraft that were spared reluctantly from the hard-pressed RAF Bomber Command — all were unsuitable for dropping paratroops, whilst some were already obsolete. The aircraft were cramped and uncomfortable for paratroops and exits could be extremely dangerous. However, it was a case of 'needs must when the devil drives', and such aircraft as the Vickers Valencia, Lockheed Hudson, Armstrong Whitworth Whitley and Vickers Wellington, to name but four of the earlier types, were used, not only to drop paratroops but also to act as glider tugs. Throughout 1942-43, requests were made by No 1 Parachute Training School at Ringway, near Manchester, for the allocation of a Dakota transport so that door jumping experience could be gained by the instructional staff. The experiences of the 1st Parachute Brigade in North Africa during November 1942 added weight to this appeal for during their operations this unit was making its first descents from USAAF C-47 Skytrains, and casualties were high because of this. Even an old or a crashed aircraft fuselage would have satisfied the PTS instructors, but the request could not be granted until September 1943.

In May 1942, Winston Churchill, was investigating the possibility of providing more aircraft for airborne forces training. The only real solution to the problem lay in increasing supplies of transport aircraft, such as the C-47, under Lend-Lease from the USA. The Prime Minister cabled President Roosevelt explaining the position and the reply was a promise of indirect help only. It was impossible to supply transport aircraft to the RAF because of the tremendous demands of the US forces, but he promised that four USAAF transport groups would be arriving in the UK during June-July 1942. These four groups would be equipped with 208 Douglas

C-47 and C-53 transports and by November 1942, it was hoped that the arrival of further groups would increase the total to 416 aircraft. On reaching the UK all these units would be available to assist the British Forces both in operations and training.

By early 1943 the first batches of Douglas Dakota Mk 1 transports for the RAF were leaving the new Douglas factory located at Long Beach, California. The first aircraft FD768 was delivered at the factory on 9 January 1943, and the second — FD769 — arrived in the UK on 11 February by the North Atlantic ferry route into Prestwick. (This aircraft eventually went to the Israeli Air Force, then to the Uganda Air Force in 1963, where it was involved in conflict.) Deliveries to the Middle East by the South Atlantic ferry route were also in progress, FD774, the seventh RAF Dakota Mk 1 arriving on the last day of March 1943. After service with 267 and 216 Squadrons, it was ditched in the Mediterranean on 9 July 1943, so had a very short life. On 1 April 1943, FD781, FD786 and FD787, were delivered to India. Ferried in twos and threes the flow of suitable transport aircraft for the RAF had begun. The RAF Dakota aircrew and ground crew were unique. The early crews in the Middle East and India were pioneers in their own right and consisted of bush pilots, airline pilots and even tea planters, flying the veteran DC-2s and DC-3s before converting to the early Dakotas. As the war in Europe progressed, many aircrew, tour expired on Lancasters, Stirlings and Halifaxes from Bomber Command, and flying boats including Sunderlands from Coastal Command, were converted on to the Dakota and sent out to the Middle East and later to assist in the Far East to the war against Japan.

The aircraft which was basically the prototype of the C-47 Dakota was first flown on 17 December 1935, by Carl Cover, from Clover Field, Santa Monica, California — the Douglas DC-3. However, let not all the glory be showered on the DC-3 airframe, for without the extensive and successful engine development by both Pratt & Whitney and Curtiss-Wright, no DC-3 or Dakota could have lifted from the runway with the greatest of ease. The development of the 1,000hp radial air-cooled engine, endowed with a high degree of reliability and a moderate fuel consumption, gave the C-47, and its many variants, the boost it had to have to generate high lift with the wings. Coupled with that was the development of 100 octane fuel, the development of the Hamilton Standard hydromatic quick feathering propellers plus instrumentation and communication equipment, not forgetting 'George' the Sperry automatic pilot. Today the Pratt & Whitney Twin Wasp R-1830-90C nine-cylinder engines are still available in large numbers, are still being overhauled, re-built and exported, to be fitted in the ubiquitous 'Gooney Birds' remaining in service around the globe.

Much discussion and correspondence has revolved around the name 'Gooney Bird'. Many say it originates in the South Pacific on the small atolls where the real Gooney bird — a king size seagull-like species — makes its home. One source claims that the 10th Air Transport Group based at Patterson Field in 1939 called their Douglas C-39 transports 'Gooney Birds' or 'Goonies'.

Eventually the C-47 was to serve the US armed forces in three major world conflicts — World War 2, Korea and South East Asia — plus playing a major role in many other policitical trouble spots throughout the world — the Berlin Air Lift of 1948 being a good example, when USAAF and RAF Dakotas carried many tons of food to the beleaguered city of Berlin. The C-47 fought with the French at Dien Bien Phu. It has been a peace keeper with the United Nations forces serving in Africa and other continents. Today it is still in the front line, there being over 60 military air arms in the world's inventory which still operate the type as a military transport, many with no plans or thoughts of a replacement — let's face it, there just ain't one . . . !

I cannot hope to list every name of the hundreds of individuals who responded to my pleas for help with this book and it would be invidious to list only a few and not all. I can only acknowledge with deep gratitude the help received from many friends and fellow aviation 'buffs' the world over.

I must mention too the spontaneous generosity and cooperation from a world-wide collection of 'Gooney Bird' and 'Dakota' crew members, air and ground. Squadron and Troop Carrier Group Associations also assisted, especially in lending rare photos from equally rare private collections brought out from their sacred foot lockers and archives. I only hope this book meets with approval; it is not meant to be a detailed history, but a fitting tribute to 'man and machine' — the latter the immortal Dakota.

An unknown admirer of the commercial Douglas transport once wrote: 'The only replacement for a DC-3 is another DC-3' which must have been brought to the notice of the US Navy Department, who had 100 of their earlier models stretched and modified into the Douglas R4D-8 'Super-DC-3' which served in the conflicts in Korea and South Vietnam. It was Dwight D. Eisenhower who once said that the C-47 Dakota belonged alongside the jeep, the bulldozer, the amphibious DUKW and the two-and-a-half ton truck as the equipment most responsible for Allied victory in World War 2. Thousands of veterans would agree. To quote an unnamed transport pilot 'You might wreck a Dakota, but you'll never wear it out'.

Arthur Pearcy
Dakota
Four Mile Bridge
Anglesey 1981

8

Less than six months after the first
flight of the first DST, the Douglas
DC-3 production line at Santa Monica
was in top gear. This photograph,
taken on 3 September 1936, shows a
line of DC-3 fuselages awaiting their
turn to be worked on. More than 800
DC-3s were produced prior to World
War 2. *Douglas Aircraft*

The
Birth of the
Douglas Commercial

Donald Wills Douglas

Above: A rare photo showing Donald W. Douglas deplaning from a C-47 Skytrain, the major product of the Douglas Aircraft Company during World War 2. On his left is Gen George C. Marshall USAAF. *Douglas Aircraft*

Donald Douglas was a design genius and his talent flowered with the Douglas DC-1 — the forerunner of the lesser known but equally successful Douglas DC-2 — and the most famous transport of them all, the Douglas DC-3.

Born on 6 April 1892, in Brooklyn, New York, the son of an assistant bank cashier, young Donald Douglas was fascinated by ships, studied hard, and passed the necessary examinations to enter the US Naval Academy at Annapolis. Before he entered the service school in the autumn of 1909, he went to nearby Fort Myer, Virginia, where the US Signal Corps was conducting acceptance trials on the Wright Brothers' flying machine, the first ever military aeroplane. He saw Orville Wright put his box-kite biplane through its paces, and apparently never forgot it.

After his resignation from Annapolis, and prior to his enrolment at the Massachusetts Institute of Technology, Douglas had attempted to join both Grover Loening and Glen Curtiss, early pioneers in the growing aircraft industry, but was turned down by both. He graduated in 1914 after two of the four years normally required, and was requested to stay on as Assistant Aeronautical Engineer, a post he occupied for only one year, but one which gave him the opportunity to work with wind tunnels, the first of their kind and size in the country. One of this fellow professors, was one Jerome C. Hunsaker, who later became Chief of the Bureau of Construction and Repairs, Aircraft Division, US Navy. Donald Douglas became Hunsaker's assistant, this playing an important part in shaping his future career in aviation. Design and construction, rather than teaching, attracted Douglas and in 1915 he joined the Connecticut Aircraft Company as a consultant. This was the beginning of his professional career. His association with the company was very brief and during August 1915 he joined the Glen Martin Company in Los Angeles as chief engineer where he designed an attack bomber for the US Army.

Donald Douglas was ambitious, and at times restless, as he wanted to be his own master and establish his own aircraft company. Despite an attempt by Glen Martin to dissuade him, in March 1920 he finally decided that he wished his children to live in the warmth of southern California, and his aircraft to fly in the same salubrious climate. That his total assets were in the order of $600 proved no deterrent. He invested some of this money in desk space at the rear of a downtown barber's shop on Pico Boulevard, Los Angeles, and commenced a search for additional capital. A friendly Bill Henry, once public relations officer with Glen Martin and now a sports writer, introduced Douglas to David R. Davis, a millionaire sportsman and flying enthusiast who was prepared to finance an aeroplane which would fly the 2,500 miles coast-to-coast non stop. So with a first order worth $40,000 to build such an aeroplane, the Davis-Douglas company was formed, and Douglas immediately summoned from the east six associates who had worked with him at Martin.

From then on the life of Donald Wills Douglas was closely associated with the history of the Davis-Douglas Co, the Douglas Company, the Douglas Aircraft Company, and the McDonnell Douglas Corporation, and with the wide variety of aircraft they have designed and built since 1920.

The eminence of Donald Douglas as a creative engineer and head of a major industrial establishment more than once was recognised by the US government and members of his own industry. Despite the many honours accorded him as a member of the top echelon in American business, he did not take the airs of industrial royalty. One incident is illustrative of that quality. On the day the board of directors of the Douglas Aircraft Company were to meet for the last time prior to the merger in 1967 with McDonnell, the huge headquarters building located just off Lakewood Boulevard, Long Beach, California, was bustling with limousines, helicopters, and busy senior executives and their aides. After the meeting, with all the VIP's departed, an elderly gentleman stepped alone out of the elevator, chatted with the security guard in the lobby and walked to his faded Mercury sedan. Donald Wills Douglas drove himself home.

President of the Douglas Aircraft Company, John C. Brizendine, describes DWD as 'a great human being as well as a giant of aviation, and if I have any hero in the world, he was it'. Donald Wills Douglas died on 1 February 1981, in Palm Springs, California, at the age of 88. He was the man who made commercial aviation possible through the Douglas Commercial series which revolutionised the airline business, and which included the DC-3 from which many military derivatives were born including the 'Gooney Bird' or 'Dakota'.

The Birth of the Douglas Commercial

The single most important date in the history of the Douglas Aircraft Company is 2 August 1932. It was on this date that Jack Frye, vice president in charge of operations with TWA — Transcontinental and Western Air, wrote letters to several aircraft manufacturers. One of Frye's letters was addressed to Donald W. Douglas, then 38 years old and president of the Douglas Aircraft Company, now located at Santa Monica, California. Others went to Curtiss-Wright, Ford, Martin, and Consolidated. The two-paragraph letter was soliciting bids for 10 or more trimotor transport aircraft. TWA's specification called for an all-metal, trimotored monoplane. Composite construction could be offered (as could a biplane) but the main internal construction, wings and fuselage, must be of metal. Recommended powerplants were the 500-550hp Wasp engines equipped with superchargers for high altitude operation, built by Pratt & Whitney. The aircraft must provide for a crew of two, pilot and co-pilot, with a cabin capable of carrying at least 12 passengers in comfortable seats, and fully equipped with the many fixtures and conveniences generally expected. The most stringent requirement reads as follows: 'This plane, fully loaded, must make satisfactory take-offs under good control at any TWA airport on any combination of two engines.' The fact that one of TWA's major airports was Albuquerque, New Mexico, located at an elevation of 4,954ft and where summer temperatures often exceeded 90°F, made this requirement difficult to meet. There was no doubt about it; here was a challenge tempting to any aircraft designer.

TWA lost a Fokker F-10A NC999E on 31 March 1931, killing all on board including the great Knute Rockne, famed Notre Dame football coach, whilst flying from Kansas City to Wichita, Kansas. This crash resulted in the Bureau of Air Commerce instructing operators of this and all other type of airliners with wooden spars and ribs to inspect the internal wing structure periodically. These inspections proved excessively costly and time consuming for the US airlines and resulted eventually in the phasing out of most wooden airliners. By 1932, resulting from this directive, TWA found it necessary to look for new aircraft.

Donald Douglas called the letter from Jack Frye 'the birth certificate of the DC ships' and deservedly so. After digesting its contents he called in his production and engineering team,

Below: The one and only Douglas DC-1-109 (X223Y c/n 1137) in TWA livery, seen parked at Clover Field, Santa Monica, California, prior to its first flight on 1 July 1933. It was originally powered by two Wright GR-1820-F3 Cyclone 700hp engines. The TWA spec called for an 85ft wing-span, low-wing, all-metal monoplane, with a max range of 1,000 miles at 190mph with 500 US gallons of fuel. Take-off weight was to be 17,500lb, including two crew, 12 passengers and 1,000lb of freight. It exceeded all expectations. *Douglas Aircraft*

consisting of J. H. 'Dutch' Kindleberger, Arthur E. Raymond, Fred Herman, Lee Atwood, Ed Burton, Fred Stineman, and Harry E. Wetzel. The Douglas team decided to take the plunge, exceed what TWA had demanded, but to use a different approach in achieving the end product. The requirement for three engines was scrapped. More powerful engines would soon be available as both Pratt & Whitney and Wright-Aeronautical had some new engines on the test blocks. Two of these were expected to do the job. The adoption of a fuselage sufficient to enable the taller passengers to stand upright in the aisle, combined with effective cabin sound-proofing, were to offer greater passenger appeal and make it more competitive. Douglas replied to Jack Frye's letter and indicated that they were definitely interested. The team's proposal was already being put on paper, and there was a name for the project — they called it the DC-1, *Douglas Commercial Model No 1*. Ten days after the receipt of the TWA specification, Arthur E. Raymond, deputy chief engineer and Harry E. Wetzel, general manager, left for New York to present the proposal. On 20 September 1932, the contract was signed in the presence of Jack Frye, Richard W. Robbins, TWA president, and Col Charles A. Lindbergh, TWA's most famous stockholder and chief technical advisor. The price agreed on for the aeroplane was $125,000 to be paid in gold bullion, and if the cost exceeded the figure, Douglas would have to stand the difference. An option clause in the contract gave TWA the right to buy all, or part of, 60 additional transports in lots of 10, 15 or 20, at $58,000 each. This figure did not include the cost of the engines. That same day Donald Douglas signed the work order at Santa Monica to start the DC-1 project and sent it down to the shops. The first transport would have to be hand built.

At the factory detailed engineering work began at once and Douglas called upon several new techniques, including extensive use of wind-tunnel tests, fuselage mock-up and independent test models for various systems such as fuel and hydraulics, to optimise the design. Work moved ahead of schedule. On 15 March 1933, TWA representatives approved the fuselage mock-up, which was about three-fifths complete. However, in the process of adding all the luxuries including sound-proofing, cabin temperature control, improved lavatory facilities and more comfortable seats, the weight had increased from 14,200lb to 17,000lb. Arthur Raymond found the answer. The West Coast representative for Hamilton-Standard propellers was Al French, who offered the recently perfected controllable pitch propellers. With these, a pilot can automatically adjust the blades so they will take bigger bites of air at take-off, giving enough added thrust to lift the heavier loads. An 11th scale model of the DC-1 was undergoing tests in the 200mph wind tunnel at the California Institute of Technology. With aerodynamic con-

figurations finalised, the fabrication process began on two aeroplanes. One was a full-scale mock-up made of wooden framework and covered with heavy paper to simulate the aluminium skin of the real aircraft. The other was the DC-1 itself. Selection of engines led to intense competition between Pratt & Whitney and Wright which respectively offered variants of their Hornet and Cyclone power plants. By April 1933, experts from the Wright team moved into Santa Monica; they set up their office on one side of the ramp, while a team from Pratt & Whitney did the same thing across the way, their products hidden behind large screens. The teams did not speak to each other for fear of divulging company secrets. However, TWA and Douglas agreed initially to install two 690hp Wright SGR-1820-F nine-cylinder air-cooled radials. To begin with fixed-pitch propellers were installed but were soon replaced by variable pitch units.

On Thursday 22 June 1933, little more than 10 months after receipt of Jack Frye's letter, the first— and only — Douglas DC-1 was rolled out of its hangar and on to the Clover Field. She looked gigantic. The fuselage was 60ft long, half as long again as a Greyhound bus. A low-wing monoplane with a wing span of 85ft, it rested on a conventional undercarriage, two main wheels on shock aborbing struts plus a small tailwheel. This was the largest land-plane configuration ever built in the United States as a twomotored monoplane design. It carried the experimental registration X223Y and the Douglas serial number 1137.

On Saturday morning, 1 July, the DC-1 was ready for its initial test flight. It was planned to fly it during the lunch hour so that all Douglas factory personnel could watch. It was bright and clear with a light west wind blowing off the Pacific Ocean. Chief test pilot Carl A. Cover, expressed satisfaction and was joined on board by Fred Herman, the project engineer. The DC-1 trundled to the east end of the runway, turned into wind and started its take-off roll. The DC-1 was airborne at exactly 12.36pm — all was well. All was well for 30sec, at which point the port engine spluttered and stopped. The pilot recovered a few hundred feet of altitude and then the starboard engine also stopped. The maiden flight was almost the last flight as the engines failed each time the DC-1 assumed its climbing attitude, and the aircraft was saved only through Cover's skilful piloting. Immediate investigation revealed that the carburettor floats were mounted in such a way that fuel flow ceased every time the nose of the aircraft was raised. Fortunately, there was nothing wrong in the design of the DC-1 and on return to flight status it proved a complete success and was subjected to one of the most rugged, extensive flight test programmes ever required of any aeroplane.

During the three months following the eventual maiden flight the DC-1 was intensively tested by pilots from Douglas, TWA and the Bureau of Air Commerce. However, the flight test programme

Left: The first Douglas DC-2 first flew on 11 May 1934. It was DC-2-112 c/n 1237 and was delivered three days later to TWA as NC13711 '301' *City of Chicago*. By October 1942 it was in India as RAF Douglas DC-2K DG477 with 31 Squadron as 'Z-Zulu', eventually being struck off charge on 8 November 1943.
Author's collection

was marked by a series of memorable incidents including the almost complete jamming of the control surfaces due to the use of the wrong type of hydraulic fluid in the automatic pilot system. There was an accidental wheels-up landing at Mines Field, the airport serving Los Angeles, when a crew member forgot to lower the mainwheels. The transport suffered a couple of bent propellers, but no structural damage.

Finally on 4 September 1933, the DC-1 was put through its most difficult test to demonstrate ability to meet TWA's most stringent requirement — a flight from Winslow, Arizona to Albuquerque, New Mexico, with one engine shut down from take-off to landing. After one of its engines had been switched off during the take-off run, the DC-1 climbed slowly from 4,500ft to its cruising altitude of 8,000ft and, single-engined, successfully flew the 280 miles between the two airports. Douglas had proved the DC-1's ability to meet all the requirements demanded by TWA in its original request dated 2 August 1932. TWA placed an initial order for 20 DC-2s, a derivative of the DC-1 with fuselage length increased by 2ft to accommodate an additional row of two seats. Take-off weight was 18,000lb with 14 passengers and 1,740lb of freight with a maximum range of 1,060 miles at 196mph with 510 US gallons of fuel. This order was placed on 4 September 1933 and the first DC-2 (NC13711 c/n 1237) was rolled out of the Santa Monica factory during May 1934, with its first flight following on 11 May, with delivery to TWA three days later. It was little thought that this particular aircraft, some eight years later, would be in use as a transport of war with the Royal Air Force in India, flown by pilots based with No 31 Squadron. By June 1934, a total of 75 of the new Douglas aircraft were on order.

The Douglas DC-1 was officially handed over to TWA during December 1933. There was an appropriate ceremony at Los Angeles Municipal Airport when the company handed Donald Douglas a cheque for $125,000. This was the beginning of a new era for the company which was to become the largest producer of commercial airliners in the world. Earlier, on 8 November 1933, the CAA granted their approval for the Pratt & Whitney Hornet-powered DC-1A and with these engines made its first flight on 6 October. Ground and air tests were extensively conducted and the Hornet engines were in and out of the DC-1 several times as various modifications were incorporated. In any event the Wright Cyclone was eventually selected.

Little was heard of the DC-1 over the next year, but it was not idle. Now registered as NC223Y with TWA, it was used as a flying laboratory over the airline's network and, occasionally, it was operated for a few scheduled passenger flights pending the delivery of the production DC-2 transports. During early 1935 it was loaned to the Department of Commerce and the US Army Air Corps to test a new Sperry automatic pilot linked to the Kreuse radio compass. During the early part of 1936, TWA used the DC-1 for high-altitude research flights. The engines were changed to Wright GR-1820-F55 Cyclones with two speed blowers, turning Hamilton Standard constant-speed propellers, plus oxygen and autopilot. The latter enabled the captain and crew to record data on engine and aircraft performance, as well as cloud and wind data above 20,000ft. At these altitudes, the aircraft was flown on instruments, as frost obscured the windows. A total of eight new World records and 11 US records for speed and distance were set with the DC-1.

During 1935, American Airlines were searching for a new aircraft to replace their fleet of Curtiss Condor sleeper biplanes in service on their trans-continental route from Boston to Los Angeles via Dallas. The airline was operating the Douglas DC-2, which was an improvement on the Boeing B-247D, but it was still not wholly satisfactory. The payload of the DC-2 with 14 passengers and the range, not enough for a flight from New York to Chicago, were inadequate. It had propeller and fin icing problems, was nose heavy, difficult to land and directionally unstable, its vertical fin area was insufficient. On handling characteristics it was described as 'a good example of a flying barn door' with especially heavy ailerons and rudder.

Above: The first Douglas Sleeper Transport (DST) made its first flight on the 32nd anniversary of man's powered flight, 17 December 1935, and is seen here in flight as NC14988 DST-144 c/n 1494. Small windows are for the upper berths. It crashed at Knobmaster, Missouri, whilst serving as a military C-49E 42-43619 on 15 October 1942. *Douglas Aircraft*

Cyrus Rowlett Smith, President of American Airlines and his Chief Engineer, William Littlewood, were both acutely conscious of the deficiences in the DC-2. Donald Douglas was approached by C. R. Smith on the subject of producing yet another successful aircraft for the airlines, and there is no doubt that emphasis was on the new project during the two-hour telephone conversation with Douglas during the latter part of 1934, and which laid the foundations of the Douglas DC-3 transport. Sir Peter Masefield in his excellent paper read for the First William Littlewood Memorial Lecture on 19 November 1971, for the first time reveals details of the development of the new aircraft:

'Littlewood's first ideas, and then more positive thinking, on the potential development of the DC-2 began in 1934. As Vice-President, Engineering, of the new American Airlines, Bill Littlewood's ideas gained impetus as he widened the thinking of C. R. Smith and with his assistant, Otto E. Kirchner. Their discussions "gelled" around the possibilities of a "wide-body", longer-range, stretched DC-2 with more powerful "G-series" Wright Cyclone engines. As the discussions developed there were three obvious requirements: 1 More payload than the DC-2 could lift — to be gained without any substantial increase in "aircraft-mile" costs and therefore at a significantly reduced "seat-mile" cost; 2 A body wide enough to accommodate berths on each side of an adequate aisle so that the new aircraft could be used for transcontinental sleeper services in succession to the Curtiss Condor biplanes; and 3 Increased range to cut out the stops between New York and Chicago — and achieve transcontinental services in four hops.'

These three basic requirements led on to a detailed examination by Bill Littlewood and Otto Kirchner, early in 1935, of the possibilities of splitting the DC-2 fuselage longitudinally through the middle, widening it by a 26in wide insert to make possible two seats on one side of the aisle and one on the other, lengthen the fuselage to gain eight rows of seats of three abreast for the dayplane (24 seats) and three double rows of berths on each side of the aisle for the sleeper (12 berths), plus two extra in a private 'honeymoon' sky room on the right of the front fuselage. In the end one row of seats was sacrificed to give more baggage space forward, thus reducing day seats to 21. The DC-3 came out with a fuselage 92in wide, and 78in high from the floor — which compared with the 66in width and 75in cabin height of the DC-2.

All this was made possible by notification from Curtiss-Wright, early in 1935, that the 750hp R-1820-F engines of the DC-2 could, they hoped, be developed into 1,000hp R-1820-G engines by the end of the year. Littlewood recalled that work started on the design of the DC-3 some 18-months before engines were available to power it. The original talks about a 'wide-body, stretched DC-2' were, clearly, wholly within American Airlines between Bill Littlewood, C. R. Smith and Otto Kirchner. Their first ideas were that the new aeroplane would be about 85% DC-2 and about 15% new, with a 50% increase in payload. If the 'aircraft-mile' costs could be held the aircraft would be able to make money. It ought to be ready for service by the middle of 1935. In the end the developed aeroplane turned out to be almost wholly new — with a wider and longer fuselage, more wing span, more tail volume with a dorsal fin to stop the 'fish-tailing' of the DC-2, a stronger landing gear and more power. It took two years to bring into service rather than the one year originally considered as possible.

But for C. R. Smith's persistence with Donald Douglas during that historic phone call, there would have been no DC-3. Douglas was reluctant to embark upon a new project at a time at which he had a full order book for the DC-2. At the end of the telephone call, C. R. had made it clear that the American would contemplate an order for up to 20 'wide-body' developments of the DC-2 if Douglas would build them and that half of the order could be for Sleeper Transports for 14 passengers and the other 10 as dayplanes with 50% payload and longer range than the DC-2 — and no 'fish-tailing'. Somewhat grudgingly Donald Douglas agreed to go ahead with a design study and C. R. said that, at the right moment, he

would send Bill Littlewood to Santa Monica to help.

Design work started right away under Arthur Raymond with basic layout under Ed Burton and aerodynamics headed by Dr Bailey Oswald. They worked in close consultation with the NACA and the Guggenheim Tunnel under Clark B. Millikan and A. L. (Maje) Klein at Cal Tech. Lee Atwood headed the stress department. All of it stemmed, of course, from the original work on the DC-1 and the DC-2 headed in 1932 by J. H. (Dutch) Kindlberger, then Vice-President Engineering of Douglas before he moved on, in 1934, to become President of the General Aviation Corporation, shortly after renamed North American Aviation Inc, of Inglewood.

On 10 May 1935, Arthur Raymond produced 'Douglas Aircraft Report No 1004' which outlined performance and weights of a 'Douglas Sleeper Transport' developed from the DC-2 to American Airlines' requirements. There were long telephone calls between Chicago and Santa Monica and, on 17 June 1935, Harry H. Wetzel (Senior Vice-President and General Manager of Douglas Aircraft, and Donald Douglas' right hand man since 1922) wrote to Bill Littlewood to quote prices for five, six or 10 DSTs at, respectively $82,000, $81,000 and $79,500 each for delivery at one a week from 15 February 1936, subject to acceptance within 10 days. Precisely 10 days later, on 8 July 1935, C. R. Smith telegraphed Douglas 'Enter our order ten model DST airplanes delivery according letter from Wetzell 27 June' and to guarantees according to Douglas Report No 1004. The order was confirmed by Douglas on 9 July and Bill Littlewood arrived in Santa Monica on 17 July to work over details 'flanked by a lawyer on one side and a purchasing agent on the other'.

There was at one time a good deal of scepticism within American Airlines about the advisability of buying the DC-3. But both C. R. and Bill Littlewood believed that the trend must be towards 'more power and more airplane' and that it was worth gambling that Wrights would come up with 1,000hp engines in time. There was no certainty. But it happened. Douglas built a

mock-up — the most comprehensive up to that time; some 15,000 man-hours were expended on it. American sent a Curtiss Condor to Santa Monica so that the sleeping berths could be studied. 'We did things much closer to the job then' said Littlewood. He and Harry Wetzel spent time lying down on the berths to prove precisely the best places for the lights. But the contract between Douglas Aircraft Company and American Airlines was not signed until 8 April 1936.

Manufacture of the first DST began just before the end of 1934. The first ground run of the engines took place less than a year later on 14 December 1935. Carrying the experimental registration X14988 it was wheeled out for a 90min engine run at noon. This first DST was, at that time, without the dorsal fin which later was characteristic of all DC-3s. It was added in March 1936 to improve stability in the approach.

The first flight of the first DC-3 — the Douglas Sleeper Transport variant — was from Clover Field, Santa Monica at 1500hr on 17 December 1935, with Carl Cover (Douglas Vice-President Sales) as pilot, accompanied by two flight engineers, Ed Stineman and Frank Collbohm, and by Jack Grant, mechanic. The flight lasted 30min and was followed by two more to bring the total time that day to 1hr 40min. The aeroplane was then flown daily from Clover Field — except for 21 December, Christmas Day, 27 and 30 December, right up to the end of the year. By 14.30hr on 31 December a total of 25hr 45min had been accumulated, mostly by Elling H. Veblen, Douglas test pilot and by M. Gould (Dan) Beard, American Airlines Engineering test pilot. According to the log-books of X14988, Carl Cover made the first three flights on 17 December and flew the aircraft again the following two days and then handed it over to Veblen and Beard with two final flights on 20 December. Only 15hr 25min were flown in January to bring the total hours to 40hr 55min by the end of the month. Between 11 and 31 January X14988 was grounded for modification to the propeller controls and exhausts. In spite of such interruptions, including a double engine change

Above: This TWA DST (DC-3B-202 X17312 c/n 1922) was photographed at the Union Air Terminal at Burbank, California on 16 April 1937, prior to delivery. During 1942 it was impressed into military service as C-84 42-57157 and returned to TWA two years later. *W. T. Larkins*

15

Above: The first Douglas DC-3 to be fitted with Pratt and Whitney engines was this DST-144 c/n 1496 seen before its first flight on 14 June 1936. The third production aircraft, during 1942 it went to the military as C-49E 42-56103, being returned to American Airlines two years later. The engines were Twin Wasp SB3-Gs. *United Aircraft Corp*

Right: Wright Cyclone engine change at Kingman, Arizona, on a TWA Douglas DC-3 DST transport during 1936. Note the rather primitive tackle used. TWA was then Transcontinental & Western Air Inc and operated a large fleet of the new Douglas Commercial transports. *Auhtor's collection*

between 18 and 26 February, test flying of the DST went on more or less continuously throughout the first four months of 1936. The second DST NC16001 made its first flight on 4 June 1936. There was thus a five-month interval between the first flights of the first and second DSTs, after which aircraft were produced at an accelerating rate — 30 in the last six months of 1936.

There was no prototype. And most of the engineering test flying continued to be done by Dan Beard of American Airlines — an example of manufacturer/customer relationship which is perhaps unique, and certainly helped to get the desired results. There were two episodes along the test flying path, either of which might have brought the project to an early end.

Between 6 and 10 January a serious problem revealed itself in that X14988 showed itself to be incapable of meeting the stipulated take-off unstick distance of 1,000ft at 24,000lb AUW. in fact, so convinced did Tomlinson of TWA become upon the likely inability of the aircraft to operate from most of the small airfields of that day, that he reported adversely on the aircraft and departed to Kansas City from Santa Monica in mid-January, in the belief that American Airlines had bought a 'clunk' and that TWA should look for more DC-2s rather than to the DC-3. By the time TWA caught up with progress it had lost valuable places on the production line to American and United. The take-off problems were real and Dan Beard himself was worried. There seemed no doubt that the Wright G-5 engines were not giving enough power. In mid-February Bob Johnson and Bill Birren of Wrights — who shared Beard's concern about take-off performance — asked for X14988 for a week during which both engines were changed and modifications were incorporated in the replacement Cyclone G-5 engines to restore the power.

According to Johnson and Birren, both old friends of Bill Littlewood and members of the Wright Aeronautical team, the crankcases of the original engines were holding churned up, pressurised, oil at high take-off rpm. The effort expended by the crankshaft in stirring up the oil was costing about 75bhp per engine. The replacement engines had fore and aft holes through the lower crankcase walls and a pick-up close to the rotating parts which forced out the oil. The power was restored. Take-off tests ran by Veblen and Beard on 28 February showed a distance of 970ft. All was well.

The second episode was on 5 March 1936 near the end of the test flying period after X14988 had been flown for 66 hours in all. The aeroplane had been ferried from Clover Field to Mines Field, Inglewood for landing and brake tests. Beard recounts that he was taking movie pictures of the runway marks out of the right cockpit window while Veblen made the landing. Suddenly he was thrown against the window as the aeroplane

Left: Father and Son. David Wills Douglas Sr with Donald Douglas Jr seen in the cockpit of a Douglas Super DC-3 transport in November 1959 when the Super Dak was a new project. The idea failed with the airlines, but benefited the US Navy who procured 100 and used them in Korea and Vietnam. *Douglas Aircraft*

Below: Unfortunately cockpit photos of many aircraft types are not always available. Depicted is an excellent view of the 'office up front' from C-47-DL 41-18523 c/n 4615. Constructed in 1942 this aircraft was used by ATC on the South Atlantic ferry shuttle during World War 2 and not broken up until September 1966. *USAF Museum*

swung violently as it touched with one wheel almost locked and the other wholly free as a result of — as was discovered later — a burst actuating cylinder. Beard sensed what had happened as the aeroplane swung off the runway and headed in a skid towards one of the hangars. There was no time to correct the swerve so he gunned the right engine in the direction of the ground loop. The aeroplane finished up with the tail within 2ft of the hangar after skidding sideways through a 4ft cyclone fence. Fortunately the damage was small and the aeroplane was flown back to Clover Field for repair. But had Beard not reacted instinctively and had the ground loop not been successful there seems no doubt that the cockpit would have gone through the concrete wall of the hangar and neither pilot would have survived — nor might the DC-3 project.

A 14-passenger day-and-night interior was installed between 6 and 22 March while the aeroplane was under repair — the 14 day seats in facing pairs and upper and lower berths to make up at night. The dorsal fin was also added to improve approach control. Just over seven weeks after the episode at Mines Field, DST X14988 c/n 1494 received its Certificate of Airworthiness on 29 April 1936. The first batch of aircraft was certificated at a gross weight of 24,000lb. The gross weight was later raised to 25,000lb and then to 25,200lb as more engine power became available. Afterwards military C-47s flew regularly at 32,000lb gross weight — with no positive single engine rate of climb.

On the day on which it received certification NC14988 was delivered to Phoenix, Arizona by Jake Moxness of Douglas Aircraft and formerly accepted there by American Airlines. The device of taking acceptance in Phoenix had been initiated by American for its DC-2s in order to avoid Californian Sales tax. It was continued for all its DC-3s. As soon as documentation had been completed NC14988 was flown back to Santa Monica by AA pilots and between 2 and 7 May completed the Department of Commerce 50hr airline proving flights between Glendale, Fort Worth, El Paso, Phoenix and Douglas. There followed a period of grounding while some 60 outstanding items were sorted out between American Airlines and Douglas Aircraft. These were finally resolved at a high level after Arthur Raymond had moved some drawing boards into the flight hangar and cleared modifications on the spot.

The third DST NC16002 flew on 14 June and was delivered on 17 June. The eighth aeroplane of the series and the first 21-seat DC-3 day plane NC16009 flew on 16 August and was delivered on 18 August. With the two DSTs delivered to Chicago by 18 June, American Airlines intensified training and some publicity and propaganda flying in preparation for the first commercial services. One of the most remarkable of these propaganda efforts was on 21 June 1936 when NC16001 was filled up to its full load of 822 US gallons of fuel and made a round trip non-stop from Midway, Chicago, to Newark, New Jersey and back to Midway in eight hours seven minutes with a standard crew plus C. R. Smith, Bill Littlewood, Bob Johnson and a few others. The aeroplane landed with some 50 US gallons remaining.

The historical records reveal that NC14988 served American Airlines named 'Texas' until 14 February 1942, when it went to TWA and just under a month later was put in military markings and designated a C-49E with USAAF serial 42-43619 and was based at Kansas City. On 15 October 1942, it was wrecked at Knobmaster near Chicago. It is coincidental that the remaining seven DST transports produced for American were also impressed into USAAF service as C-49E transports. The Douglas Commercial Three had gone to war.

Right: Interior cabin view, looking forward uphill to the cockpit, of a Douglas C-53 Skytrooper taken on 27 January 1942. The bucket type seats possibly gave birth to the name 'Ole Bucket Seats' one of many nicknames given to the Dakota transport. *P. M. Bowers*

Immaculate Douglas C-47-DL
41-18604 c/n 4765 seen after roll-
out at Long Beach, California on
10 October 1942. It was delivered to
Daggett, California for fitting out, then
went to Ladd, Alaska on
23 December 1942, and then via the
ALSIB route to Russia on 31 January
1943 under Lend-Lease.
Douglas Aircraft

Into Uniform

The US Airlines go to War

Above: To ensure the US transport needs were met, the airlines became immediately involved in World War 2. This American Airlines DC-3 was built as a Model DST-144 NC16002 c/n 1496 in June 1936, impressed as Douglas C-49E 42-56103 in June 1942 and by July 1944 was back with the airline as a freighter and advertising war bonds. *American Airlines*

Below: Likewise TWA DC-3s served the military, flying in military livery with the crews having commissioned ranks in the USAAF. However, this Douglas DC-3-277C (NC28310 c/n 2251, built in July 1940) missed the impressment but carried the challenge that 'Victory is in the Air — BUY BONDS'. It crashed in a thunderstorm during 1944. *TWA*

Above right: Superb photo of United Air Lines Douglas DST-A-207 NC18109 c/n 1957. Delivered during August 1937 with a right hand door, this aircraft became a C-48B (42-56090) during June 1942 and was used as a VIP transport by Gen Mitchell. It was struck off charge at Bergestrom AFB during July 1943. *P. M. Bowers*

Right: The single Douglas C-48 — 417-7681 c/n 3256 — was drafted into the Army Air Corps before delivery to United Air Lines as NC25612 DC-3A-197D. It carries the two-star insignia of a major-general and the fin markings indicate it is aircraft '2' of the 1st Staff Unit based at Bolling Field, Washington DC. It is seen here at Oakland, California in June 1941. The aircraft in the left background is a Boeing 247, which lost out to the Douglas Commercial for transport supremacy in the mid-1930s. *P. M. Bowers*

Top: The one and only C-52C, 41-7701 c/n 4136. Ex-DC-3-201G NC33630 for Eastern Air Lines, this aircraft was drafted at Santa Monica and is seen here in its warpaint livery at Oakland, California on 6 December 1941. On 13 September 1941, it was based at Mitchell Field and was condemned at Bowman Field, Kentucky, on 16 September 1942. *P. M. Bowers*

Above centre: Very unusual markings are seen on this Douglas C-49K 43-2016 c/n 6340 drafted during January 1943, ex-DC-3-G202A NC30038 intended for Eastern. It served with the North Atlantic Wing of Air Transport Command from 17 October 1943 and carries the ATC insignia on the fuselage band. *W. T. Larkins*

Above: Just about to touch down at the Santa Monica facility with Douglas built Flying Forts in the background is this Douglas C-48C, 42-23827 c/n 2147. Ordered by KLM as DC-3-194H PH-AKH during December 1939, it was delivered to United on 24 April 1940. Impressed by the military on 15 March 1942, it was used by ATC on the North Atlantic Wing and returned to United Air Lines on 5 December 1943. *P. M. Bowers*

Left: A US Navy airline impressment was Douglas R4D-4 Bu No 07003 c/n 6349, which was originally built as DC-3A-477 NC34955 for Pan American Airways. It was one from an order for 10 for PAA which were all drafted into the Navy as R4D-4s. This one was impressed on 4 January 1943, and soldiered on until March 1965 when it was finally retired. It is depicted in Naval Air Transport Service livery. *US Navy*

Into Uniform

The DC-2 entered military service as early as 1934 when the US Navy bought five aircraft (s/n 9630-9622, 9993, 9994). Given the model designation R3D-1, they were assigned to US Marine Corps at Quantico, Virginia. They provided performance advantages so far removed from the veteran Curtiss R4C Condor two-motor biplanes or Ford Tri-Motors monoplanes they replaced that, henceforth, the USN maintained a strong preference for the type — so much so that there are still a handful of Super DC-3 or C-117Ds in USN service.

The US Army Air Corps bought its first DC-2 in 1935 and was impressed enough to order a number which received various designations — the most numerous being the C-33s (redesignated C-39 in 1938). Other early military users of the DC-2 were the Republicans in the Spanish Civil War and Finns in November 1939. But it was to be in USAAF (and also in RAF) colours that the Douglas Commercial was to make its name, and the fact that it did so was to some extent through luck.

Early US Army Air Corps attempts to develop transport aircraft had produced no satisfactory model, and, in spite of redoubled efforts, no successful design was produced during the war years. So, inevitably, the USAAF turned to civilian models already in production. The early standby, and indeed the most dependable aircraft within its capabilities throughout the war, was undoubtedly the Douglas DC-3, known alternatively, according to its special modification, as the C-47 and C-53. Long successful in civilian passenger service but already obsolescent at the time of Pearl Harbor, the twin-engined DC-3 had many features ill-suited to the convenient handling of bulky freight and its payload was too light for the new tasks. But it was flyable under almost any condition, was easily maintained and, above all, was in production by the Douglas Aircraft Company.

The US Army Air Corps had only been a nominal customer, whereas the US Army Air Force, so named on 20 June 1941, became the largest of the Douglas DC-3 military derivatives. In addition to handling Lend-Lease contracts for the Allies and orders for R4D transports for the US Navy Department, it acquired some 10,000 aircraft through direct contracts for new aircraft designed specifically for military operations and built at the Long Beach, Oklahoma City and

Santa Monica factories, through purchase of civil orders still under construction in the Santa Monica factory, and through impressment of Santa Monica built DST/DC-3 airliners.

On 16 September 1940, the first contract — AC15847 — was placed for fully militarised versions, when 147 C-47 transports to be built in the new Long Beach factory were ordered. The first aircraft off the production line was 41-7722 completed on 23 December 1941 with Douglas c/n 4200*. During 1941 the Oklahoma City factory was added as a second source of production, with 1,900 C-47A-DK transports being ordered under contract AC28405. The Santa Monica factory became involved in military production when on 24 June 1941, the USAAF ordered 92 C-53 transports under contract AC18393. No Douglas C-47 transports were built at Santa Monica.

The Douglas Aircraft Company built a grand total of 10,044 DC-3s on production military contracts at its three factories, with deliveries between October 1941 and 31 August 1945. Santa Monica built a total of 378 C-53s. Long Beach built 4,285 C-47/R4Ds. Oklahoma City built 5,364 C-47/R4Ds and 17 C-117s. The 538 prewar DST/DC-3s built at Santa Monica and the 28 DC-3Ds converted after World War 2 from un-completed orders at Oklahoma City brought the total DC-3 production in the USA to 10,665.

An interesting sidelight on this production is provided by Sir Peter Masefield who visited the Douglas Aircraft factories during World War 2:
'I visited the Douglas production lines at Santa Monica, Long Beach and Oklahoma City, in the USA during August/September 1943. It was interesting to see the hive of activity at all three

Above: Long before the days of paved level runways, a landing on soft ground with a large transport aircraft was always hazardous. Depicted is a Douglas C-33 transport which has its wheels sunk up to the hubs. The red and white horizontal rudder stripes were in use from early January to 15 May 1942. *P. M. Bowers*

Right: The unofficial hybrid 'DC-2½' designation commenced with the early Douglas C-33, the first true cargo transport variant of the DC-2. Note the larger DC-3 type fin and rudder. This immaculate transport is seen fresh out of the Douglas factory awaiting test flight on 26 August 1936. *Douglas Aircraft*

Below: The Douglas C-33s soon went into warpaint with serial numbers being added to the fin during January 1942. The four digits '6084' interpret this as 36-84 the personal transport of Commanding General of the Spokane Air Depot fitted with curtains at each window. The photograph was taken at Felts Field on 28 February 1943. *P. M. Bowers*

Bottom: Another hybrid. Douglas C-39 38-509 c/n 2066 Model DC-2-243 from the huge Fairfield Air Depot, seen landing at Burbank, California during June 1941. The transport has a DC-2 fuselage and outer wing panels, DC-3 centre wing section and tail unit. *P. M. Bowers*

plants and C-47s in serried ranks alongside production shops for Boeing B-17s and Douglas single-engine dive-bomber aircraft production. The impressive thing was the enthusiasm of the workforce, of whom quite a large proportion was women and girls, most, in those days, with their hair done up in brightly-coloured handkerchiefs and all bright overalls as well. The work's hangars were so well camouflaged against the possibility of Japanese air attack on the West Coast, that one drove up to what looked like a palm tree-lined suburban street, only to find, when one came close, that it was the painted side of a workshop.

'I flew on one or two production clearance test flights. I remember that there were generally only a relatively few detailed snags to clear before a second flight cleared the aircraft for collection by ferry pilots. The interiors were, of course, bare of furnishings and specialist equipment was usually installed later, at a modification centre, were much of the work could be done in the open. The C-47 production was part of a remarkable aircraft production war-effort in the United States, which, by 1943, was reaching its peak. There has certainly been nothing like it before, or since.'

With the military forces of the Allies during World War 2 the military version of the DC-3 became known as Dakota, the name continuing the British tradition of assigning geographical names to transport types and representing a clever acronym of the letters DACoTA — Douglas Aircraft Company Transport Aircraft. Mark numbers were assigned only to transports corresponding to genuine military C-47s and C-53s received under Lend-Lease. The Dakota Mk I was the equivalent of the C-47-DL; Dakota Mk II the C-53-DO; Dakota Mk III C-47A-DL/

DK; and the Mk IV the C-47B-DK. The impressed DC-3s were named simply Dakotas — a name which after the war was used to describe any DC-3.

During World War 2 the Royal Air Force received a total of 1,928 Dakotas including: eight ex-civil DC-3s (LR230 to LR235, MA925 and MA926) acquired from US airlines by the British Purchasing Commission; 53 Dakota Mk Is (FD768 to FD818, HK983 and HK993); nine Dakota Mk IIs (FJ909 to FJ912, HK867, MA928 and MA929, and TJ167 to TJ170); 962 Dakota Mk IIIs (FD819 to FD967; FL503 to FL652; FZ548 to FZ698; KG310 to KG809, TS422 to TS427, TS431 to TS436); and 896 Dakota Mk IVs (KJ801 to KJ999, KK100 to KK220, KN200 to KN701, KP208 to KP279, TP181 and TP187). A number of these transports were transferred during the war to other Commonwealth and Allied forces including the Royal Canadian Air Force and to British Overseas Airways Corporation.

In spite of the loss of more European orders for the DC-3 with the outbreak of hostilities on 3 September 1939, the Douglas Aircraft Company continued to receive substantial airline orders, primarily in the US but also in other still peaceful areas of the globe. When the Japanese attacked Pearl Harbor, the military was able to obtain an immediate supply of transport aircraft by taking over civil DC-3s and DC-3As then on the production line at Santa Monica. A total of 137 aircraft was involved, and as they had been ordered to different airline specifications, and were powered by a variety of both Wright and Pratt & Whitney engines, they became assigned under 22 different designations with the Air Corps. Twelve of them were taken over but

remained undesignated. (See table listing these transports.)

The military impressment of DST/DC-3 variants directly from the US airlines provided a third source during the early part of World War 2. A total of 93 of these aircraft was obtained in this manner, but many were leased back for use on government approved routes. More often than not, however, an aircraft was not necessarily leased to the airline from which it had come.

Since March 1941, the US Navy and US Marine Corps have operated a total of at least 567 military transport versions of the DST and DC-3 series, the Navy Department directly ordering only 78 of these. All other Douglas R4Ds —

Right: Spartan, but with a certain clean mechanical allure, this is the interior of a 12-passenger Douglas C-39 transport taken on 11 February 1939. The radio operator's position is opposite the cargo door. The differentiated right and left hand seats are contoured for seat-pack parachutes. *Douglas Aircraft*

Below: An external crane could be fitted to the Douglas C-39 and the huge cargo door was in two sections; the narrow aft part could be opened separately. The cargo being lifted is addressed to the Air Corps Supply Officer, Sacramento Air Depot, California, and contains aircraft parts from the Douglas Aircraft Company then located at Santa Monica, California. *Douglas Aircraft*

as the Navy version was originally designated — were ordered on behalf of the Navy by the USAAF, or were subsequently transferred from the USAAF inventory. The Navy models were designated as follows:

R4D-1 The first 66 aircraft were ordered under a US Navy contract, whilst an additional 40 came via USAAF contracts. Generally similar to the C-47-DL it differed only by the installation of some Navy instruments and communications equipment. Powered by Pratt & Whitney R-1830-92s and delivery began in February 1942.

R4D-2 Two ex-DC-3-388 transports ordered by Eastern Air Lines taken over by the US Navy whilst still under construction, and despite the designation became the Navy's first variant. Lacking the reinforced floor and cargo door of the R4D-1, they were used as staff transports and later as VIP flagships. They were powered by Wright R-1820-71s and corresponded to the USAAF C-49 transport.

R4D-3 These 20 personnel transports were Douglas C-53-DOs transferred from the USAAF.

R4D-4 Ten DC-3-447s taken over by the US Navy whilst still under the original order for Pan American, and still being constructed. Used as personnel transports and generally similar to the USAAF C-53-DO.

R4D-5 Originally contained in a USAAF C-47A-DL order, a total of 81 were transferred to the US Navy. Later supplemented by 157 C-47A-DK transports. Many of this model were modified for special tasks.

R4D-6 Corresponding to the USAAF

Above: The single Douglas C-41, the first ever military Douglas DC-3, serial 38-502 identified as a Model DC-3A-253 c/n 2053. It was delivered to Gen Hap Arnold on 11 October 1938, as a military executive aircraft with military radio installed. The Pratt & Whitney R-1830 Twin Wasp engines were given the Army designation R-1830-21. This C-41 accumulated 2,739 flying hours up to April 1945. *USAF*

Left: A few KLM Douglas DC-3s escaped the invasion of Holland in May 1940, and operated from Whitchurch, Bristol, alongside BOAC. This DC-3-G2-194 PH-ALI c/n 1590 *Ibis* became G-AGBB and on 1 June 1943, was shot down over the Bay of Biscay by a Luftwaffe Junkers Ju88 with the loss of 17 lives including the British actor Leslie Howard. Note the neutrality markings 'KLM HOLLAND' carried under the fuselage. *Real Photographs*

Below left: A very very rare bird — one of three Douglas C-39 transports which escaped from the Philippines to Australia and used by Australian National Airways (ANA) with US military insignia and Australian radio call-sign VH-CDB. The aircraft was used by 36 Squadron RAAF from 24 June 1943. *P. M. Bowers*

Above: Impressive World War 2 view of the Long Beach production line depicting a neat row of Douglas C-47A-75-DL Skytrains. The line on the left of the photo is more or less complete and includes 42-100875 c/n 19338 to 42-100880 c/n 19343. The immediate follow on batch included RAF Dakotas TS422, 423, 432, 433. *Douglas Aircraft*

Above right: Ground-floor view of the Douglas production line which has reached the stage where the Pratt & Whitney R-1830-90B Twin Wasp engines are installed. This power plant contributed greatly to the success of the C-47 Dakota, and today in the UK, Twin Wasps are rebuilt and overhauled for export to Dakota operators. *IWM*

Centre right: When the 2,000th C-47 Skytrain — C-47A-50-DL 42-24256 c/n 10118 — rolled off the Long Beach production line, Douglas publicist Joe Messick autographed the fuselage. By the end of the workshift hundreds of workers had scrawled their signatures on every inch of the aircraft. Although the chalk was rubbed off before the USAAF would accept it, many 'Rosie Riveters' managed to get their names and addresses in the wheel wells and hidden compartments. Mechanics in the war zones who found these sent 'pen pal' romance letters from all over the world. *Douglas Aircraft*

Bottom right: Line-up of completed Douglas C-47 Skytrains for the USAAF awaiting test flight. After testing they will go to a depot to be fitted out for the theatre of operations intended — usually one test flight was sufficient before acceptance by the military. *Douglas Aircraft*

C-47B-DK, under which designation they were ordered, the US Navy obtained a total of 150 of these transports.

R4D-7 In addition to the transport models mentioned, the US Navy operated 41 of the R4D-7 trainers obtained from a USAAF contract for TC-47B-DKs.

The initial C-47 transports were designed and intended for the transportation of troops, either combat or medical evacuees, medium and light cargo support for airborne assaults. However, the air transport configuration of the C-47 proved to be so successful that it soon became a jack of all trades in the USAAF and the armed forces of the Allies including the RAF. It must be remembered that the C-47 has served the US Armed Forces in three wars. The C-47 that was basically the DC-3 airframe progressed from an initial weight of approximately 18,300lb to a gross weight of 29,200lb. As the tactics for airborne warfare evolved, so did the multitudinous functions of the C-47. The demand far exceeded the supply and so to eliminate the shortage, the USAAF built the Douglas Oklahoma City facility as a secondary source of production. Mention must be made of the major sub-contractors who supported the massive production programme involving the Douglas C-47. These were Beech, Cessna, A. O. Smith, Murray Body, Fleetwings, Pullman-

Standard and many more. All these vendors were located in the mid-west of the USA.

When it is considered in retrospect, the capacity of the Douglas Long Beach factory complex as originally constructed is almost beyond the comprehension of the layman. During the month of May 1945, more than 415 C-47 transports were delivered by the factory to the USAAF. This is no small programme when it is considered at that time the factory was also building approximately 120 Boeing B-17 Flying Fortress aircraft per month. All aircraft built were ready for delivery by air, and, in the case of the C-47s, after completion were taxied around the edge of the airfield to the Air Transport Command base at Long Beach Army Air Field, ready for their ultimate destination.

It is believed that most RAF Dakotas were ferreid to Daggett in California before delivery to 45 Group RAF located in Canada. Here the transports were readied for delivery across the Atlantic, either to the UK by the northern route, or to the Middle East and India by the southern Atlantic route. Capt Robert F. Soule USAAF was a member of a ferry party who picked up three Douglas C-47B-20-DK Oklahoma City built transports (43-49919, 43-49936, 43-49947) at Baer Field, Fort Wayne, on 4 February 1945, for delivery flight by the southern Atlantic route

Top right: The first Douglas DC-3s used by the US Navy were two VIP R4D-2s diverted from an Eastern Air Lines order at Santa Monica. This one is ex-DC-3-388 NC28389 and was the first for the US Navy. Here it is seen with BuNo 4707 c/n 4097 at San Francisco during March 1941 in the standard prewar colours and markings. It was based at Anacostia, Maryland. *W. T. Lanrkins*

Centre right: The Douglas DC-3 production commenced at Santa Monica and continued there until the end of the C-53 Skytrooper production. This Douglas C-53D-DO, 42-68818 c/n 11745, is parked outside the factory in front of the elaborate camouflage 'hill', complete with simulated city streets, housing and trees, built over the factory during the early part of 1942. *Douglas Aircraft*

Right: Early Douglas R4D-3s were originally Army Air Corps C-53 Skytroopers. This unidentified R4D-3 was photographed at National Airport, Washington DC during early 1942 with the navy green warpaint, rudder stripes and stars on both wings. *US Navy*

Below: Typical World War 2 US Navy base scene of activity with two Douglas R4D-1s parked on the ramp — 7-R-109 and 7-R-106 from VR-7 Squadron of the Naval Air Transport Service (NATS). On the left is a Navy PBY Catalina coded 4-J-13. *US Navy*

to Pomigliano, Italy, where they arrived on 16/17 February 1945. They were for use by the 62nd Troop Carrier Group, 52nd Troop Carrier Wing. The first mentioned C-47 43-49919 flown by 'Bob' Soule, had only $4\frac{1}{2}$ hours flying time on the airframe when picked up.

Brief details of the USAAF C-47 models are as follows:

C-47-DL Named Skytrain by the USAAF, this was the first fully militarised version of the DST/DC-3 series. Powered by two 1,200hp Pratt & Whitney R-1830-92s. Had a large two-panel cargo door on the port side incorporating in its forward portion a standard door, and reinforced fuselage floor with tie-down fittings. An astrodome was added behind the flight deck. Cargo hooks were fitted beneath the wing centre section to carry large items for their release by parachute. Another mod was the removal of the tail cone to mount a cleat for glider towing. The normal crew consisted of pilot, co-pilot and radio operator, and the transport could carry 6,000lb of cargo, or up to 28 airborne or parachute troops in folding canvas seats on the sides of the cabin, or 14 stretchers and three nursing attendants. Total of 965 produced at Long Beach.

C-47A-DL and C-47A-DK The C-47A was the most prolific version, and, alone accounted for almost 50% of the complete Douglas production of DSTs, DC-3s and military derivatives. Long Beach produced 2,954 and Oklahoma City 2,299. The C-47A differed from the C-47s primarily in being fitted with a 24V instead of 12V electrical system and had improved cabin heating.

C-47B-DL and C-47B-DK Powered by 1,200hp R-1830-90C engines with two-stage blowers and fitted with improved heaters, the C-47Bs were evolved for high-altitude operations such as the Hump route in the China-India-Burma theatre of operations. Long Beach produced 300 C-47Bs and Oklahoma City 2,932. The last C-47 delivered was a C-47B-50-DK (c/n 34409 USAAF serial 45-1139) which was handed over to the USAAF on 23 October 1945.

TC-47B-DK This model was produced at Oklahoma City in parallel with C-47Bs and the 133 TC-47Bs built were equipped as navigational trainers, with the appropriate specialised equipment.

C-53-DO The 221 C-53 Skytroopers were troop transports built at Santa Monica, powered by 1,200hp R-1830-92s. They did not have the large cargo loading door, reinforced floor or astrodome of the C-47. They were fitted with 28 fixed metal seats and a towing cleat for use as a glider tug.

C-117A-DK Towards the end of World War 2 the USAAF, with sufficient operational transports, felt a need for less spartan staff transports. A total of 17 C-117A transports was built at Oklahoma City in 1944/45 with a 21-seat airline type interior. Powered by two R-1830-90Cs with two-stage blowers, but had no large cargo door or reinforced floor. The final Douglas C-117A (C-117A-DK c/n 34318 USAAF serial 45-2561) accepted by the USAAF on 29 December 1945, was the very last new derivative of the famed DST/DC-3 to be built.

Douglas DC-3 transports impressed direct from airlines

USAAF Desig	No of aircraft	Engines	USAAF Serial
C-48B-DO	16	R-1830-51	42-38324, 42-38325, 42-38326, 42-56089, 42-56090, 42-56091, 42-56098, 42-56099, 42-56100, 42-56101, 42-56102, 42-56609, 42-56610, 42-56611, 42-56612, 42-56629.
C-48C-DO	9	R-1830-51	42-38258, 42-38259, 42-38260, 42-38327, 42-78026, 42-78027, 42-78028, 44-52990, 44-52991.
C-49D-DO	5	R-1820-71	42-38256, 42-43624, 42-65583, 42-68860, 44-52999.
C-49E-DO	22	R-1820-79	42-43619, 42-43620, 42-43621, 43-43622, 43-43623, 42-56092, 42-56093, 42-56094, 42-56095, 42-56096, 42-56097, 42-56103, 42-56104, 42-56105, 42-56106, 42-56107, 42-56617, 42-56618, 42-56625, 42-56626, 42-56627, 42-56634.
C-49F-DO	9	R-1820-71	42-56613, 42-56616, 42-56620, 42-56621, 42-56623, 42-56628, 42-56633, 42-56636, 42-56637.
C-49G-DO	8	R-1820-97	42-38252, 42-38255, 42-56614, 42-56615, 42-56630, 42-56631, 42-56632, 42-56635.
C-49H-DO	19	R-1820-97	42-38250, 42-38251, 42-38253, 42-38254, 42-38257, 42-38328, 42-38329, 42-38330, 42-38331, 42-57506, 42-65580, 42-65581, 42-65582, 42-68687, 42-68688, 42-68689, 42-102422, 44-83228, 44-83229.
C-52D-DO	1	R-1830-51	42-6505.
C-84-DO	4	R-1820-71	42-57157, 42-57511, 42-57512, 42-57513.

Impressed Douglas DC-3 transports

USAAF Desig	No of aircraft	Original customer	Douglas Spec No	Engines	Seats
C-48-DO	1	United	DC-3A-377	R-1830-82	21
C-48A-DO	3	—	DC-3A-368	R-1830-82	10
C-48C-DO	7	Pan Am and associates	DC-3A-414	R-1830-51	21
C-49-DO	6	TWA	DC-3-384	R-1820-71	24
C-49A-DO	1	Delta	DC-3-385	R-1820-71	21
C-49B-DO	3	Eastern	DC-3-387	R-1820-71	21
C-49C-DO	2	Delta	DC-3-386	R-1820-71	28
C-49D-DO	6	Eastern	DC-3-389	R-1820-71	28
C-49J-DO	34	sundry	DC-3-454	R-1820-71	28
C-49K-DO	23	sundry	DC-3-455	R-1820-71	28
C-50-DO	4	American	DC-3-396	R-1820-85	21
C-50A-DO	2	American	DC-3-401	R-1820-85	28
C-50B-DO	3	Braniff	DC-3-397	R-1820-81	21
C-50C-DO	1	Penn Central	DC-3-391	R-1820-79	21
C-50D-DO	4	Penn Central	DC-3-392	R-1820-79	28
C-51-DO	1	Canadian Colonial	DC-3-390	R-1820-83	28
C-52-DO	1	United	DC-3A-398	R-1830-51	28
C-52A-DO	1	Western	DC-3A-394	R-1830-51	28
C-52B-DO	2	United	DC-3A-395	R-1830-51	28
C-52C-DO	1	Eastern	DC-3A-402	R-1830-51	29
C-53C-DO	17	sundry	DC-3A-453	R-1830-92	28
C-68-DO	2	—	DC-3A-440	R-1830-92	21
Undesignated	12	Pan Am and associates	DC-3A-414	R-1830-92	28

Above right: 'Join the Navy and see the world' — the picturesque scenery of the Aleutians provides a backcloth for this Douglas R4D-1 from VR-4 Squadron and coded 4-R-150. The aircraft was possibly carrying supplies and personnel to some outlandish US Navy base during World War 2.
US Navy

Right: Superb landing shot of a Naval Air Transport Service Douglas R4D-6, BuNo 50821 c/n 15431, on final approach to the naval air station at Oakland, California on 1 April 1946. This aircraft remained in service, being reworked and rebuilt as a Douglas R4D-8 Super-Dak.
W. T. Larkins

In USAAF Service

C-47 Skytrains from the 438th Troop Carrier Squadron, under Col John M. Donaldson, lined up at RAF Greenham Common. The first two aircraft in line are from the 89th TC Squadron — C-47A-70-DL 42-100766 c/n 19229 4U-D *Lilly Bell II* and 42-100776 c/n 19239 4U-N. *IWM*

316th Troop Carrier Group

During World War 2 the 316th Troop Carrier Group participated in all but one of the major airborne operations executed in the Mediterranean and European Theatres of Operations, winning three Presidential Unit Citations and receiving credit for nine campaigns.

The 316th came into existence under Col Jerome B. McCauley on 14 February 1942, when its Headquarters and HQ Squadron plus two of its tactical squadrons — 36th and 37th — were activated at Patterson Field, Ohio. The group was brought up to its full complement of four tactical squadrons on 15 June when the 44th and 45th Squadrons were activated and assigned. Nine days later the Group moved to Bowman Field, Louisville, Kentucky, where it carried out its training programme. On 9 August the unit moved to Lawson Field, Fort Benning, Georgia, where it was brought up to its full aircraft strength of 52 — Douglas C-47 Skytrains and C-53 Skytroopers — and it commenced training with airborne troops. A move to Del Valle Air Base, Texas, on 29 September enabled the group to undergo six weeks of further intensive training with airborne units; these units including the 82nd Airborne Division.

On 10 November 1942, the 316th received its overseas movement orders. Five days later the air echelon departed from Texas, en route to the Middle East. By 25 November the air echelons of HQs and of the 36th and 37th Squadrons were at Deversoir, Egypt, and that of the 45th Squadron at Ismailia, Egypt. The 44th Squadron was held temporarily at Accra on the Gold Coast, from where it flew two missions, transporting personnel and equipment to the Belgian Congo, and it finally arrived at Ismailia on 4 December. By the time the group's ground echelon, which left the USA on the USS *Mariposa* on 20 December 1942, arrived in Egypt on 1 February 1943, the crews with their Douglas transports had more than two months' of operations behind them. Upon arrival in Egypt the air echelons found themselves in a very active theatre. The battle of El Alamein had only recently been won by the British Eighth Army, with considerable assistance from the US 9th Air Force — to which the 316th was assigned upon its arrival in Egypt. By the end of November the front line was more than 700 miles away, to the west of Benghazi, and was moving every day. The extended supply lines were placing a heavy burden on both land and sea transportation facilities. In addition the RAF were very short of suitable transport aircraft. Consequently, the 316th Group, the only USAAF troop carrier organisation then in the Middle East, had its work cut out for it.

From November 1942 until May 1943, the 316th supported the British Eighth Army, the RAF, and the 9th Air Force in the massive Allied sweep across North Africa into Tunisia. The group's Douglas transports carried aviation fuel, oil, bombs, ammunition, food and other supplies. Frequently the transports landed on fields which only a few hours earlier had been occupied by the enemy. On many occasions casualties were evacuated on the return flight. On 11/12 December 1942, six transports of the 45th Squadron carried 11,664gal of aviation fuel from a landing field near Tobruk to an advanced airfield and evacuated 77 casualties. From 8 December 1942 to 24 January 1943, the group's aircraft carried more than 3,000,000lb of freight, including more than 500,000gal of fuel, and evacuated more than 1,400 casualties. In April they carried something like 3,000,000lb of freight and transported approximately 7,000 passengers.

One reason for the almost unbelievably rapid advance of the Allies across North Africa was the

Below: Three NCO pilots of the 36th Troop Carrier Squadron at Del Valle Army Air Base, Austin, Texas, in November 1942, just prior to their long flight to Cairo, Egypt. Left to right: S/Sgt Elmer Jackson, S/Sgt George Quisenberry — aircraft commander of '5' *Jiminy Cricket* — and S/Sgt Dick Welter.
316 TC Group

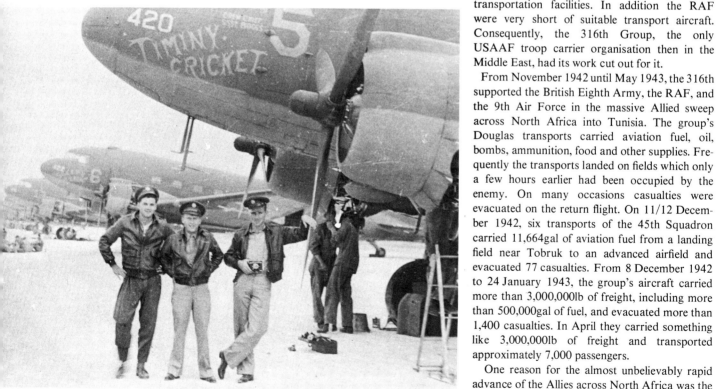

high degree of mobility of air force units and the continuous air support given to the ground forces. The 316th Group provided an invaluable service in helping to keep air force units, particularly fighter units, within range of the front line. In an incredibly short space of time, the Group moved one RAF fighter wing four times. During the advance on Tripoli, bulldozers worked all night amidst enemy artillery fire to level a landing field torn up by the enemy, and shortly before dawn the first 316th Douglas C-47 brought in sufficient supplies to allow the 57th US Fighter Group with its Curtiss P-40 aircraft, to operate against the guns which had been responsible for the shelling. The Group received commendations from both British and American commanders for the magnificent work it did in the Egyptian-Libyan campaign. One of its Distinguished Unit Citations was included in part of this work.

Approximately a week before the Axis troops in Tunisia surrendered on 13 May 1943, HQ 316th Troop Carrier Group and the 36th, 44th and 45th Squadrons — less detachments — moved to Nouvion, east of Oran in Algeria, to commence training for Operation 'Husky' — the invasion of Sicily. In May 1943 the Allies in

North Africa had only limited experience with airborne operations, but the 'Husky' plan called for a series of large-scale, night airborne operations. The planned operations presented troop carrier units with serious night-time problems, including assembly, formation flying and navigation. Consequently, the 316th Group, along with other troop carrier units, spent the period from mid-May to late June 1943 in an intensive training programme in which the emphasis was placed on finding answers to these problems. At the end of the training period the 316th moved to an airfield near Enfidaville, south of Tunis, from which it participated in the 'Husky' airborne operations.

The 316th supplied Douglas transport aircraft for both the main airborne operations on the night of 9/10 July and the reinforcement mission on the night of 11/12 July. Hampered by poor visibility and buffeted by strong winds, the unit's formation of 33 aircraft found it tough going on the first mission. It missed the island check-points in the Mediterranean, and instead of making landfall on the southern coast of Sicily, came in over the eastern coast, near Syracuse. The lead aircraft turned west towards the dropping zone, near Cela, but the formation became badly dispersed

and dropped their paratroops, including the airborne task force commander, all over southern Sicily. The group lost two aircraft on this mission.

The second 'Husky' mission was the ill-fated one, during which the friendly ground and naval gunfire took a sizeable toll of troop carrier aircraft. The object of the operation was to drop paratroops at Parello, an abandoned airfield near Gela. The first two flights of the lead group followed the prescribed course, and made their drop squarely on the objective. However just as the following squadron passed over the coast, one nervous gunner — to this day unidentified — opened fire. Almost instantly, machine guns and anti-aircraft batteries ashore and afloat opened up along the entire length of the invasion beaches. The remainder of the airborne operation was a nightmare, as many heroic pilots took frantic evasive action, flashed recognition signals and attempted to push on to the dropping zone. The 316th Group, flying as the last element, lost 12 out of 35 aircraft dispatched and had 37 casualties. Six pilots of the group returned to base with their loads, convinced that to go on was suicide. The unfortunate incident was the result of a series of shortcomings, including an inadequate fire control system, imperfections in airborne radar identification facilities (IFF), and lack of aircraft identification training. These obviously would have to be improved before another airborne operation. Moreover, although the withering surface fire was chiefly responsible for the failure of troop carrier aircraft to find their proper dropping zones on the second 'Husky' mission, the total airborne phase, which included missions in which the 316th did not participate, revealed a need for greater training in night formation flying, the development of pathfinder tactics, and the introduction of new aids to navigation.

Reorganisation of the 316th Group required by the losses sustained in the invasion of Sicily continued in August. Lt-Col Burton R. Fleet took over command on 12 August 1943. Training, particularly for new crews, was the chief task. However, by mid-August, an airborne operation in connection with the approaching invasion of Italy had become a confirmed commitment, resulting in the 316th being involved in an inten-

sive training programme with the 82nd Airborne Division. This training was orientated towards eliminating as many as possible of the undesirable features of the 'Husky' operations. The training was carried out in North Africa, but during the first week of September the 316th moved its own personnel and equipment to Mazzara, Sicily, and assisted in moving airborne troops to Sicily, from where the airborne operation would be launched. During the first half of September the detachments which had remained at Fayid in Egypt, plus the 37th Squadron, which since May had provided troop carrier services for the 9th Air Force, rejoined the Group in Sicily.

Several airborne operations, including a drop near Rome, were planned in support of the invasion of Italy. However, for a variety of reasons including unexpected enemy strength in the projected dropping zone, unsuitable terrain and the doubtful tactical value of the planned operations, the operations were cancelled. On 12 September, while the troop carrier and airborne units were waiting for an eventual assignment, the Germans launched a strong offensive which quickly became serious enough to demand reinforcements for the US Fifth Army. Consequently, on 13 September the army commander called for paratroops to be dropped some six miles south of the Sele River. That same night, within 15 hours of the initial request, some 1,300 troops were carried to the battle front. The 316th Group did not participate in this first reinforcement mission, but its Douglas aircraft led one of the formations in a similar mission on the following night. As the result of a strict and effective anti-aircraft control order, and employment of visual and radio communications which assisted both in navigating the prescribed course and in locating the dropping zone, the operation was very successful. The 316th lost no aircraft and virtually all of the paratroops were dropped in or immediately adjacent to the designated DZ.

This was the last of the group's Mediterranean airborne operations. Until February 1944, the 316th carried supplies and equipment from North Africa to Italy and evacuated casualties. Its base was now at Borizza, Sicily, and its aircraft were often on task in places as far away as Egypt.

Meanwhile, during August 1943 the group had been transferred from the 9th Air Force, which was moving out to the UK, and became part of the 12th Air Force. However, plans for the invasion of northern France — Operation 'Overlord' — called for a large-scale airborne operation. In preparation for this operation the 316th moved out from is base in Sicily on 12 February 1944, the first element of the group arriving at AAF Station 489, RAF Cottesmore, Rutland three days later. It was destined to remain at this UK base for the rest of its World War 2 career. Upon arrival in the UK, the group was once more assigned to the 9th Air Force as part of the huge 9th Troop Carrier Command.

Intensive training took place during April and May, the 316th being involved in a programme which included joint manoeuvres with airborne forces. These exercises included orientation flights for paratroops, the dropping of paratroops on specified dropping zones, and the towing and releasing of loaded gliders. In addition to the work with airborne units, every effort was made to develop individual and unit proficiency and techniques by conducting ground school programmes, training flights, practise glider tow formations, cross-country navigation, night flying, and formation flying. During the group's preparation for 'Overlord', it suffered a tragic loss. On the last comprehensive manoeuvre with airborne forces on Operation 'Eagle', Lt-Col Burton R. Fleet, the Group Commander, with his crew and the members of another aircraft crew were killed in a collision. On 13 May 1944, Col Harvey A. Burger took over command of the 316th.

During the night of 5/6 June, 1944, the invaluable experience gained in the Mediterranean and the extensive training in the UK paid a handsome dividend. In the pre-dawn airborne assault that heralded the invasion of western Europe, the 316th dropped troops from the US 505th Parachute Infantry Regiment near Ste Mere Eglise. As a result of previous experience and vastly improved pathfinder and marker equipment techniques over those used in Sicily, the drop was an outstanding success. The group's transports dropped more than 1,200 troops on or reasonably close to the dropping zone. No air-

craft were lost although about a dozen were damaged. On the following day the 316th provided transports for a supply mission to the same area. This too, was successful, but it was marred by a take-off collision in which one pilot was killed and two aircraft destroyed. For a few days after the airborne operation there was no opportunity for transport support. However, by using hastily constructed airstrips in the bridgehead the group soon returned to the freight hauling and evacuation business. Despite the generally poor weather in July the 316th transported 796,559lb of freight and 1,756 passengers and evacuated 2,704 casualties. It flew a few supply and evacuation missions during August to newly captured airfields, but during the month a considerable amount of time was devoted to servicing transports and moving to airborne concentration centres in preparation for further airborne operations. The speed of the Allied advance was such however, that several planned operations — the crossing of the Seine, for example — were never required.

Late in August 1944, the 9th Troop Carrier Command was relieved of its assignment to the 9th Air Force and became part of the newly formed First Allied Airborne Army. These high level administrative changes did not effect the 316th, which remained assigned to the 9th Troop Carrier Command and to its parent 52nd Troop Carrier Wing, but these changes did suggest that a renewal of airborne operations was imminent.

Top: Typical scene in the Middle East after Alamein, as C-47 Skytrains attempt to keep up with the advance of the ground forces. The first aircraft in this line is C-47DL 41-38704 c/n 6163, the second is 41-38749 c/n 6208. The latter survived the war and was sold to Scottish Aviation as G-AGWS and took part in the Berlin Airlift during 1948. *Douglas Aircraft*

Above: Pre-Normandy invasion glider tow practice over the English countryside with a C-47 Skytrain from the 316th Troop Carrier Group, towing a Waco CG-4A Hadrian glider. *316 TC Group*

Anticipation of increased activity as a part of the new FAAA was well founded, and in September came the huge airborne drop in Holland — Operation 'Market Garden' which involved airborne landings to secure the bridges over the Lower Rhine at Arnhem and the Waal at Nijmegen.

On D-Day, 17 September, the 316th flew two missions of 45 aircraft each and dropped 1,360 paratroops of the US 82nd Airborne Division in the vicinity of Nijmegen. These troops dropped by the group had the task of taking bridges across the Maas-Waal Canal, and their dropping zone was therefore as close to the bridge as possible. Despite intense ground fire, the pilots pushed on and dropped the troops on or within a mile of the prescribed DZ. On the following day, in its first glider towing mission of the war, the group dispatched 82 Douglas C-47 Skytrains, each towing a Waco CG-4A Hadrian glider loaded with reinforcements. All gliders were towed to the combat area, but because of the lack of experience in glider operations and faulty interplane communications, most of the gliders were released prematurely. No aircraft were lost. Unfortunately, after 19 September, bad weather badly hit scheduled reinforcement flights, resupply missions, and seriously curtailed the entire Operation 'Market Garden' plan. Almost every day after D+1 the 316th was briefed for

missions to the assault area, but not until 23 September, did the weather clear sufficiently to permit the group to fly its second glider operation. The Nijmegen operation was largely successful but the disaster to the British 1st Airborne Division of Arnhem meant that Operation 'Market Garden' failed to achieve its objective as a whole.

After Arnhem, the 316th Troop Carrier Group reverted to its routine freight hauls and evacuation missions. Throughout the next few months the flights were handicapped by bad weather. Nevertheless, on virtually every flyable day some of its transports were busy with missions to the continent. Supply and evacuation operations dominated the group's activities through February 1945. March 1945, opened with a series of practice paratroop drops, which indicated that yet another airborne operation was in the offing. As further evidence that something big was being planned, the first half of March was involved in an almost constant shuttle between depots in the UK and airfields in France, towing gliders and hauling airborne equipment. On 20/21 March 1945 crews ferried their aircraft to RAF Wethersfield in Essex, where the airborne troops were concentrated. On 22/23 March crews were briefed for the airborne mission — Operation 'Varsity', a paratroop drop on the east side of the Rhine in the vicinity of Wesel in Germany, to assist in a large-scale crossing of the river by Allied troops. On D-Day, 24 March 1945, 316th Group, transported British paratroops for the first time, provided a total of 79 aircraft, in two serials of 39 and 40. In contrast to conditions existing during earlier airborne operations, the weather was near perfect for Operation 'Varsity', and the operation was one of the most successful airborne drops of World War 2. Troops were dropped safely, accurately and on time. One reason for this was that the Germans withheld their fire during both the approach and drop. However, as the aircraft made their 180° turn away from the target, the enemy opened up with intense and accurate light flak which took its toll of the relatively slow, unarmed, low-flying Dakotas. Of the 240 aircraft making up the formation with which the 316th flew, anti-aircraft fire destroyed 13 of which three were from the 316th Group. Seven crash-landed in friendly territory and over 100 more were damaged. The combat career of the 316th Troop Carrier Group during World War 2 ended shortly after Operation 'Varsity' and late in March 1945, the group was scheduled for an early return to the USA. In April the departure date was fixed for 7 May, but it was seven days later that the group left RAF Cottesmore and the UK. It arrived at Camp Kilmer, New Jersey on 24 May and on the following day moved to Pope Field, Fort Bragg, North Carolina, still equipped with Douglas C-47 Skytrains.

Top left: Preparations for some of the post D-Day invasion follow-on missions involving large numbers of British-built Airspeed Horsa gliders. The photo is believed to have been taken at RAF Cottesmore, Rutland, the UK home base of the 316th Troop Carrier Group. *316 TC Group*

Bottom left: Photographed at RAF Goxhill, Lincolnshire, during 1944 is this Douglas C-47A-50-DL 42-24269 c/n 10131 from the 36th Troop Carrier Squadron, coded 6E-'C for Cocoa'. This transport survived the war and was flown back to the USA. *P. H. T. Green*

Below: After experiences in North Africa and Sicily, the 316th Troop Carrier Group developed new techniques including that of using 'Pathfinder' lead aircraft for formation para-drops. Depicted is C-47A-20-DK 42-93255 c/n 13146 from an unidentified unit with its under fuselage radar bin extended. *USAF*

The North-West Ferry Route to Russia

Left, top to bottom:

The great open expanse of Alaska was mostly virgin territory. Here C-47A-35-DL 42-23805 c/n 9667 is seen flying over the barren wasteland of the north. This Skytrain is fully loaded with cargo, including external parapacks fitted under the fuselage and wings. This aircraft is currently still flying. *Author's collection*

Seen parked at Whitehorse, Yukon, Alaska, is C-47A-90-DL 43-15732 c/n 20198, bearing the insignia of the Alaskan Division of the huge USAAF Air Transport Command. The aircraft rear end is finished in red to aid Search & Rescue in snow-covered territory. *Author's collection*

Very reluctantly the USSR allowed a small number of USAAF personnel and aircraft, including C-47s, to be based in Russia in support of shuttle bombers en route to targets in Japan. This C-47A-30-DK, 43-48258 c/n 25519 *Lady Helen*, was based at Poltava, Russia when this photo was taken in March 1945. *R. C. Jones*

The addition of skis to the undercarriage of the ubiquitous 'Gooney Bird' posed no problem to the performance, and in postwar years for Arctic and Antarctic use the wheels were removed and replaced by skis. Depicted is a drab-finished C-47B-35-DK 44-77152 c/n 16736 equipped for use in Alaska. *Logan Coombs*

Typical Siberian environment in which to operate a Russian Air Force C-47 supplied under Lend-Lease. The Skytrain is a C-47B-25-DK 44-76376 c/n 15960. It is assumed that the dogs and sleds were carried in the Douglas transport. *P. M. Bowers*

Right: Rare photos depicting a Douglas C-47 Skytrain supplied under Lend-Lease to the USSR, but modified for use by Aeroflot with a starboard door, in place of the normal port double cargo doors. Photo was taken at RAF Northolt. *R. J. Ruffle*

Below: Photo taken in Alaska, at Fairbanks, depicting a late World War 2 Oklahoma City-built Dakota C-47B-45-DK, 45-1047 c/n 17050, factory new, awaiting a ferry crew from the USSR to take delivery. Over 700 Douglas C-47 Skytrain transports were supplied to the USSR under Lend-Lease. *Logan Coombs*

Southern Combat Air Transport

In response to an SOS for additional logistic support from beleaguered US forces in Guadalcanal, following the battle of Savo Island, on 23 August 1942 a contingent of 15 Douglas R4D-1 aircraft from Marine Squadron 253 flew from San Diego, across the Pacific, to New Caledonia. From this outpost they proceeded to operate the 880-mile route to Henderson Field, Guadalcanal as fast as aircraft could be loaded. Unarmed against the danger of Japanese fighter attack, flying over water and navigating by dead reckoning without ground aids — except perhaps for the headlights of a Jeep at night — more than 1,000 flights were completed between 1 September 1942 and 1 February 1943. Outward loads consisted mainly of petrol and ammunition; inward loads of sick and wounded — 18,000 in all.

The operation was given permanent recognition under the name of Southern Combat Air Transport (SCAT), and expanded to the extent that 72 movements were recorded in one day. The initial troop carrier element of the 13th Air Force was the 13th Troop Carrier Squadron equipped with Douglas C-47s. These were assigned as needed to the joint USN/USMC/USAAF organisation known as SCAT. They began using the air strip at Torokina on 9 December 1943 and elements of the 13th Troop Carrier Squadron moved into Sansapor, New Guinea in the second half of August.

SCAT was one of the tools of Admiral Halsey, Commander Air South Pacific (COMAIR-SOPAC). Rear Admiral George Van Duers US Navy Retd, Halsey's Chief of Staff remembers: 'The unarmed DC-3s of SCAT ran regular schedules between New Zealand, Noumea, Efate, Espiritu Santo and Guadalcanal. As we built or captured fields up the Solomon chain the line was extended to them. Most flights combined passengers and cargo. When operations required, SCAT planes made all sorts of special deliveries of material and personnel. For instance during a critical period in 1942 they carried drums of aviation gasoline to Guadalcanal to keep our handful of defending fighters in the air. SCAT DC-3s had two extra gas tanks in the cabin, just aft of the cockpit bulkhead. Oval in section, about six feet long they were of some black, supposedly bullet proof material. They rested on shaped

Below: Of paramount importance to Gen MacArthur's and Admiral Nimitz's island-hopping campaign in the Pacific was the Gooney Bird's ability to fly in critical material that could not wait shipment by sea. A mixture of SCAT-operated Marine, Navy and USAAF Douglas C-47s is seen here at Pira Field, Bougainville, in support of strikes against Rabaul. The second C-47 in line is C-47-DL 41-38614 c/n 4642.
US Marine Corps

athwartship timbers. A six-inch plank nailed to the timbers between the tanks was a catwalk to the cockpit. On one occasion, because I had to go and the plane was full of medical evacuees, I made the four or five-hour trip from Guadalcanal to Espiritu sitting on that plank with my back against one tank and my legs draped over the over. A most uncomfortable ride. Aft of those tanks the sides were lined with bucket seats which could be folded to give more deck space for cargo. Even when the seats were full, some cargo was lashed to the deck between them.

'SCAT pilots were drawn from the Army, Navy and Marines. They did a phenomenal job in spite of being mostly just out of flight school and woefully lacking in general flight experience. On one trip to Guadalcanal, for instance, I was invited into the second pilot's seat and enjoying flying the aircraft. We ran into the equatorial front which was never far from Guadalcanal. To my surprise the first pilot made no move to take the controls away from a passenger he had never seen before. After I flew through the front I talked to him and found he had never flown on instruments. That evening I told my boss I wanted to fly myself on all future trips in the area! SCAT pilots were all fascinated too with what they called "transport landings". They were making knots with the tail high when they rolled their wheels on the runway and tramped on the brakes. These landings felt smooth but limited the plane's ability in forward areas for they seldom got the wheels on the mat before mid-field. Hence they constantly wanted longer strips.

'Shortage of experience, attempts to exceed their ability, and youthful high spirits caused some accidents. For instance, on a beautifully clear day a plane with a load of passengers out of Bougainville for Guadalcanal roared over a Russell Island air strip a few feet above the ground. Over water, just beyond it a gas tank ran dry, before the pilot could shift to a full one the plane hit an off-lying reef and killed all hands. In spite of a few such accidents SCAT performed essential services in a highly commendable way. Without their DC-3s and their willing young fliers the Solomon campaign would surely have taken longer, cost more lives, or possibly failed.'

Marine Capt Grant W. McCombs, an original member of SCAT, whilst on leave in California, asked to meet the man responsible for the design of the C-47 and told Donald Douglas, 'There isn't a Marine in Guadalcanal who doesn't credit the C-47s with saving the island for us more than once. Take, for instance, that day when Japanese dive bombers blew up a ship which had rushed in gasoline two days after the enemy had destroyed our fuel dumps. That meant there was no gas on the island and no way our fighter planes could get up. They called up the C-47s and we started flying gas in, 600-gallons at a trip. That kept up for a week before surface ships got in. That was the only reason our fighters and dive-bombers were able to get aloft'.

M/Sgt Walter E. Gemeinhardt USMC Retd writes:

'It so happens that back in 1943 I worked with SCAT a good bit, and knew a lot about that operation. I was a young Marine then, and a member of the 3rd Marine Amphibious Corps of which SCAT was a section. We had an Air

Left: A US Navy Douglas R4D-1 transport of SCAT takes-off from the narrow and short runway strip at Treasury Island in the Pacific. The runway ends in an 85ft drop into the ocean. When landing against a strong wind on a strip such as this, the tendency was to make a high approach because of the down draught off the end of the runway. *US Marine Corps*

Delivery Unit, and SCAT was part of "Cactus Air Force" — we made many cargo hauls up the "slot", also parachute drops. My first flight was in support of the second Battle of Bougainville — we were based at Henderson Field on Guadalcanal. We had mixed crews, sometimes Navy, Army Air Corps or Marine pilots and crew members likewise. The RD4s and C-47s were pool aircraft, mostly USAAF owned.

'We had many hairy adventures in those days, like flying with a load of 105 powder bags, right up to the gunnels — we threw away the book and disregarded the "red line". Guess we were all expendable in those days. I recall the pilot, who like the rest of us was bare footed, walking over all that powder and saying "Hell if anything happens, none of us will ever know what hit us" — how very true that was. Many drops were made to Nigi (New Zealand) troops deep inside Bougainville. These were silent giant Fiji blacks of a New Zealand regiment. They did the finest job of throat cutting on the Japs that I have ever heard of. One day, we were nearly shot down when we made a low pass over the Jap's bivouac area, dropping a load of supplies by mistake. Our

aircraft was riddled and the jump master and both pilot and co-pilot were injured. I recall most of our aircraft had girls — nude of course — painted on them, and a name to go with it. On this day I believe we were in the "Vulgar Virgin" — she survived the shoot out and continued flying for some time after.'

For the retaliatory invasion of Guadalcanal in August 1942, all land-based aircraft of the USAAF, US Navy and Marine Corps, plus the Royal New Zealand Air Force — comprising about 291 aircraft — was commanded by COM-AIRSOPAC. Eventually three air strips were constructed on Espiritu Santo and four on Guadalcanal, including the partly-built Henderson Field, all playing a major part in the ensuing campaign. SCAT with its C-47s carried cargoes which included virtually every conceivable item used by Allied units in the Pacific Theatre of Operations. When the lift included urgent medical evacuees, jeeps, oxygen bottles, fighter aircraft belly-tanks, flamethrowers, fresh meat and food, medical supplies, ammunition, mail and troops, the gross load limit was often exceeded by a ton. On occasions, the overload exceeded the gross weight limit applicable to sister aircraft flying with various US airlines by as much as two tons.

Writer Private Dave Wilburn USMC, in a wartime issue of *Douglas Airview* wrote:
'A Marine Corps R4D was first to land at Green Island, north-west of the Solomons and second in at Emirau Island in the Bismark Archipelago. They participated in the Munda push, transported parapacks to be dropped to the Marines below. One of the R4Ds came overseas on 1 August 1943, following a long flight from Camp Kearny, California, to Tontouta, New Caledonia, and was immediately put into service. On a flight between Guadalcanal and Espiritu Santos, this aircraft was lost for three hours in a storm. The aircraft battery cell had blown out, leaving the instruments useless. With a cargo of stretcher patients aboard, the navigator was as bewildered as the crew, but, with amazing good fortune, they completed the flight. By July 1945, this R4D was flying on its fourth complete change of engines, and its tenth complete tyre change. Another R4D was taken straight from the Long Beach production line as SCAT was in the midst of rapid expansion. Following its commission to active duty on 10 March 1943, this aircraft became a familiar sight as Marine Corps pilots set it down in the Carolines, Admiralties, Solomons, Russells, Hollandia, New Guinea, Auckland and Sydney. Like the other R4Ds in the group, it lifted an average gross weight of 28,500lb on each flight. In the beginning of the Munda campaign, when Seabees (Navy Construction Battalions) were grading out the shell and bomb pitted landing strip, it flew in from Guadalcanal with nearly two tons of badly needed supplies. Three weeks after Smar was invaded and the Seabees were grading

Below: SCAT transports often carried auxiliary fuel tanks in the cabin, in addition to cargo and passengers. This photograph, taken to the rear of a C-53 Skytrooper on 3 January 1942, shows four auxiliary tanks with plank mounted to enable personnel to visit the 'boys room' at the rear. *Douglas Aircraft*

Bottom: Battle scene at Yontan Airport, Okinawa, after the Japs made an attack with transports laden with special attack troops. The wreck in the foreground is the remains of Douglas C-47B-15-DK 43-49402 c/n 15218, also listed in the records of US Navy R4D-6 BuNo 50803. The C-54 Skymaster wreck is 42-72385. *US Marine Corps*

the mud and coral landing strip, it flew in with a precious cargo of jettisonable belly-tanks for USMC Chance Vought F4U Corsair fighters. Three Japanese 'Betty' (Mitsubishi G4M) Navy bombers caught the R4D on the ground at Manus Island, Bismark Archipelago. One of the bombs exploded within 30-yards of it, tearing a hole in the nose, ahead of the pilot's feet. In less than 18 months it had logged a total of 1,900 hours and flown 285,000 air miles.'

Jay Wright recalls his service in the US Navy in the Pacific:

'In 1943-44 I was attached to CASU 19 (Carrier Aircraft Service Unit) in the Solomons. During our tour we were based at three locations: Binika Island in the Russell Group and Segi Point and Munda — both on New Georgia Island. It was whilst at Segi Point, from the end of March through May 1944, that I had my closest contact with SCAT. Segi Point was a true backwater of the war. It was a 2,200ft strip of crushed coral with the jungle at one end, and the open sea at the other. At one side was a bluff about 200ft high and the other side was bordered by a lagoon. Our job was to service any US Navy type aircraft that came in, and there weren't very many. I recall working on USAAF P-38s and P-39s which squeezed themselves on to the strip. The short strip usually gave USAAF types trouble — the approach was made over the jungle and many a plane was deliberately groundlooped to keep it from going into the water at the end of the runway. The only transport aircraft we ever saw were from SCAT — olive drab Douglas C-47s with standard troop interior with seats that folded to provide more cargo space. The crews were a mixture, the crew-chief or flight engineer was always a USAAF NCO. The pilot and co-pilot were mixtures of Army, Navy and Marine officers. SCAT flew a regular schedule through the Solomons, extending as far as Australia, where the crew-chiefs did a thriving business in Aussie whisky at 50 dollars a bottle. In any event — as far as we were concerned, they brought the most important events of our lives: mail and movies. Also I know that if we needed a part for an airplane we would put in an order to our supply department, and a few days later it would show up on the SCAT flight.

'Shortly before our arrival at Segi Point, a SCAT C-47 blew a tyre during their deliberate groundloop and stuck a wing into an anti-aircraft gun revetment, damaging the wing panel beyond repair. The C-47 was parked in our area on arrival and was still there when we left. The story goes that they attempted to fly a replacement wing panel up from New Caledonia by slinging it under the belly of another C-47; en route they hit bad weather and cut it loose to drop into the ocean. They then took a second panel and loaded it in a crate across the bow of a Navy APC (a 110ft wood auxiliary boat). Again heavy weather was encountered and waves coming over the bow

smashed the crate and the wing panel beyond repair. Apparently that was the last wing panel for that particular side of the C-47 in the South Pacific.'

In a typical four weeks' operations report, one SCAT group logged 2,400 hours of combat flying in 948 flights, carried 1,320,848lb of freight, 543,629lb of mail, 7,034 passengers and 198 medical evacuees. The grand total of passenger, mail, cargo and medical evacuees, over the typical four-week period, equalled 610,051 ton-miles. Twenty per cent of this amazing figure involved instrument flying conditions and was accomplished by a hundred or so transport pilots averaging 24 years of age and 60 hours of transport flying within combat areas per month.

When the Solomon campaign ended in 1944 the remnants of SCAT and a Marine Air Wing were located at Bougainville and were transferred to the Southwest Pacific Command. By the end of the Pacific war, one SCAT group embraced a distance of 3,360 statute miles, employing 14 landing strips and operational stations and engaging 550 pilots and 825 crew members.

Below: US Troop Carrier Command used the motto 'You Call — We Haul'. This photograph shows a SCAT C-47 dropping supplies to US engineers constructing an airstrip on Bougainville island in the South-west Pacific theatre of operations. *Douglas Aircraft*

The Directorate of Air Transport

Top: Douglas C-39 (equivalent to a DC-2-243 model) from a batch of 32 delivered to the USAAF, seen at Seven Mile Strip, Port Moresby, New Guinea on 19 August 1942. The aircraft is VH-CCG — USAAF 38-508 — c/n 2076. *Australian War Memoria!*

Above: Australian troops unload C-47-DL 41-18697 c/n 6103 '57' from the 6th Troop Carrier Squadron at Wau, after flying supplies from Port Moresby, New Guinea during April 1943 *USAF*

Above right: Douglas C-47-DL 41-38676 '62' *Swamp Rat II* from the 6th TC Squadron, 374th TC Group, based at Ward's Drome, near Port Moresby, seen with a fighter escort of Bell P-39 Airacobras from 41st Fighter Sqn, 35th Fighter Group, during April 1943. This aircraft survived and was last heard of in Nigerian AF. *USAF*

Centre right: These troops, the first to be relieved of combat duty, are from 163rd Infantry Regiment, 41st Division, and being flown out from Dobodura, New Guinea to Port Moresby from Strip 4 on 10 July 1943. *US Army*

Bottom right: US 503rd Parachute Infantry Battalion landing in New Guinea. Several of the parachutes — white for paratroops, coloured for supplies and ammunition — are seen in various stages of opening, swinging the men at extreme angles, and very close to the ground. Some of the C-47s have their undercarriages partially lowered. *Douglas Aircraft*

Above: Douglas C-47A-35-DL 42-23887 '362' c/n 9749 from the 433rd TC Group, prepares to taxi out for take-off at Finschhafen airstrip, New Guinea, on 13 December 1943. The Republic P-47 Thunderbolts are from the 348th Fighter Group. This transport survived the war and stayed in Australia. *USAF*

Left: The 5th Air Force set up Air Freight Forwarding Units. Here an old, wingless, C-47 wreck is seen at the edge of Seven Mile Strip for practice loading and unloading. Time studies quickly showed the result: at first it took 45 minutes to load a jeep, but after a few days the time was down to two-and-a-half minutes to load and two minutes to unload.
Australian War Memorial

The Assault on Europe

Top right: A very rare photograph of C-48B-DO 42-56102 (c/n 2222, originally built as a Douglas DST-A-207B and registered with United Airlines as NC25682) seen visiting RAF Knettishall, Suffolk, during 1944. Col William B. David, Commander 388th Bombardment Group, is seen on the extreme right of the photo, with back to camera, while Col Curtiss E. LeMay greets the unknown two-star generals who have disembarked from the VIP aircraft. *Boardman C. Reed*

Centre right: Col Charles H. Young, Commanding Officer of the 439th Troop Carrier Group, in the cockpit of his lead-ship (C-47A-80-D 43-15159 c/n 19625) at Balderton, near Newark. *The Argonia* was named by Col Young after the small town of Argonia, Sumner County, Kansas, where he was brought up. *Col C. H. Young*

Below: 439th Troop Carrier Group at Upottery Field, Taunton, Devon on 29 May 1944, on the last practice mission before D-Day. The same airplanes and formation were used on D-Day. *The Argonia* was first in line coded D8-Z. *Col C. H. Young*

On 16 October 1943, the US 9th Air Force was reactivated in the United Kingdom, and along with it a new organisation, the 9th Troop Carrier Command. The original cadre came from HQ 1st Troop Carrier Command, and the new 9th TCC was formed under the command of Brig-Gen Benjamin F. Giles — under it was placed the 50th Troop Carrier Wing commanded by Brig-Gen Julian M. Chappel fresh from the USA accompanied by personnel with three years of troop carrier operations behind them. Assigned to the wing were the 315th Troop Carrier Group under Col Hamish McLelland and with the 34th and 43rd Squadrons only, units which had been in the European theatre with the 8th Air Force since December 1942. The 434th Troop Carrier Group under Lt-Col Fred D. Stevers, and the 435th Troop Carrier Group, both from the USA also joined the wing.

February and March 1944 witnessed the arrival of the rest of the major units to make up the 9th Troop Carrier Command. The 436th TC Group under Col Adriel N. Williams arrived on 4 February, and the 53rd TC Wing under Brig-Gen Maurice M. Beach arrived at RAF Greenham Common on 22 February. In a general reorganisation that was completed in March the 53rd TC Wing took over most of the groups in the 50th TC Wing. This included the newly arrived 437th TC Group under Col Cedric E. Heigdens, the 438th TC Group under Col John M. Donaldson, and the 439th TC Group under Col C. H. Young. Also during February 1944, the 52nd TC Wing arrived from Sicily with nine months of combat experience behind it under the command of Brig-Gen Harold L. Clark, and took up its HQ at RAF Cottesmore on 17 February.

With this wing were four groups — the 61st, 313th, 314th and the 316th, the latter also being based at Cottesmore, and being unique in that it was the only group of the old 9th Air Force — ex-Middle East — to become part of the new organisation. The remaining groups to arrive in the UK included the 440th, 441st and 442nd. All units were equipped with the Douglas C-47 Skytrain and the C-53 Skytrooper transport.

The gradual improvement of the UK weather in March 1944 allowed Troop Carrier Command to expand its intensive training. The March diary of a squadron from the 435th TC Group based at RAF Welford in Warwickshire, contained the following entries:

2 March: 12 aircraft and one Pathfinder in night paratroop drops, troopers simulated.
3 March: 12 aircraft with other squadrons on a resupply mission.
7 March: 8 aircraft formation flying — 2 hours.
12 March: Jumped 79 troopers.
15 March: 13 aircraft in paradrop mission, 213 troops and 79 parapacks.
20 March: Paradrop with engineers and some British units.
23 March: Manoeuvres for Winston Churchill, Dwight D. Eisenhower and guests.
25 March: 11 aircraft on drop mission — dropped 123 troops.
27 March: 10 aircraft and 10 gliders in tow formation, morning and afternoon.

The Troop Carrier Wings carried out combined and larger exercises. On 15 March some 50 aircraft participated in Exercise 'Thrust' with the 6th British Airborne Division. The aircraft took off at 2000hrs and flew to the DZ located near Winterbourne Stoke, Wiltshire, where drops were made between 500 and 800ft at 110mph. Five days later an unusually large exercise took place involving 279 aircraft and 154 Airspeed Horsa gliders. However bad weather over the DZ prevented jumping. Earlier in the month, the 435th TC Group, had carried out three large scale exercises, all of which were unsuccessful, and during a parapack drop on 10 March the 435th completely missed the target. These exercises and others revealed the need for more extensive practice in airborne operations.

Despite the drab olive, grey and green finish of the Dakotas which served with the 9th Troop Carrier Command, the addition of squadron codes and ident letters, some up to 4ft high, plus the application of personal art work on the nose, made the aircraft bright and unique in more ways than one. On the eve of D-Day — 5 June 1944 — 24-inch black and white invasion stripes were painted completely round the mainplanes outboard of the engines, and around the fuselage but not over the US national insignia. The upper stripes were removed two or three weeks later in common with other US aircraft types. The area art of the cockpit was used to apply combat mission symbols denoting particular operations by the aircraft.

In preparation for future operations such as 'Overlord' and 'Neptune' — the invasion of Europe — there was a gradual movement of all 9th Troop Carrier Command aircraft to three main centres. The most northerly embraced inland airfields — three in Lincolnshire and one each in Rutland and Northants. The second centre was made up of four airfields in Berkshire, and one in Wiltshire, and the third centre was near the English Channel with two airfields in Devon and two in Somerset.

All 14 groups of the 9th TCC were to take part in the opening round of the assault on Europe. Their aircraft were to deliver paratroops and

Top left: The 9th Troop Carrier Command used the Waco GC-4A glider at night, and the heavier British Airspeed Horsa in daylight. Depicted is a C-47A-70-DL 42-100770 c/n 19233 coded 4U-H from the 89th RC Squadron, 438th TC Group, seen just after take-off from Greenham Common towing a Horsa glider. *IWM*

Top right: Airborne troops wait to board C-47s, from the 61st Troop Carrier Group, initially based at RAF Barkstone Heath, Lincolnshire. The first aircraft is from the 59th TC Squadron. *IWM*

Above centre: The 34th and 43rd Troop Carrier Squadrons, 315th Troop Carrier Group, had been in the UK since December 1942, attached to the US 8th Air Force. Depicted are two Waco CG-4A Hadrian gliders being towed by C-47s from the 34th TC Squadron near their base at Stanhoe, King's Lynn, Norfolk during mid-1944. *C.G.Voegelin*

Above: 1-Lt Donald G. LePard, 91st TC Squadron, 439th TC Group, flying C-47A -75-DL 41-100847 c/n 19310 in No 2 position on the starboard wing of the Group Commander Col Charles Young during a return flight from a paratroop drop at Groesbeek, Holland on 17 September 1944. *Col C. H. Young*

Right: C-47s from the 439th TC Group loading paratroops of the US 82nd Airborne Division on 17 September 1944, at Balderton Field, Newark. The C-47 on the left with the dustbin antenna is *The Argonia*.   *Col C. H. Young*

Below: Paratroops from the 370th Engineer Battalion, 82nd Airborne Division, ready to load on board *The Argonia* at Balderton, Newark on 17 September 1944. *Col C. H. Young*

Bottom: US Engineers lay down metal strips shortly after D-Day somewhere in France. The steel matting was known as Somerfield Tracking, or Pierced Steel Planking — PSP — and served for many years giving hard wear and tear. *RAF Museum*

gliderborne infantry of the 82nd and 101st Airborne Division on six drop or landing zones in close proximity to St Mére Eglise. From there the troops would seize bridges, roads and other key points to assist the inland progress of the troops landed on Utah Beach. First despatched were six pathfinder serials — there were three aircraft to each serial, except one which had four. Their task was to drop pathfinder teams in each of the drop zones, these teams would mark each landing zone in preparation for the remainder of the troops. All six drops were accomplished.

Whilst the pathfinders were operating, 821 C-47s and C-53 aircraft, plus another 104 towing Waco CG-4A Hadrian gliders were ready to be despatched in 28 serials from 14 airfields in the UK. The first to take-off were from RAF Greenham Common — the C-47 Skytrains from the 438th TC Group, taking off at 11-second intervals. The leader was the CO Col John Donaldson flying *Birmingham Belle* which was airborne at 22.48hr 5 June 1944. As the aircraft took off they formed into serials, then into wings. Two crews from each group had been specially trained at the Pathfinder School to lead their groups within visual distance of the DZ's. From wing assembly areas the armada headed for the command departure point — 'Flatbush' — where they descended to 1,000ft and then to 500ft as they headed over the English Channel, along a 10-mile wide corridor. At 140mph, with navigation and cabin lights shrouded, they passed over a naval vessel checkpoint — 'Gallup' — in mid-channel, and then flew on to a turning point off the west coast of the Cherbourg peninsula — 'Hoboken' — where the troop carriers turned east and climbed to 1,500ft and experienced light flak from the Channel Islands. The flak grew more intense as the aircraft reached the mainland at the point — 'Muleshoe'; at this point the aircraft dropped down to 700ft and reduced speed to 125mph. As 'Birmingham Belle' reached her DZ her radio man, S/Sgt W. Wilson was wounded by flying shrapnel. Then the speed was lowered to 110mph for the drop, and as the drop zone was

identified the troops jumped — the time was 00.16hr, 6 June 1944. With their cargoes delivered the C-47s headed for the coast north of the DZs, to a point known as 'Paducah', then north to 'Spokane', before turning west to 'Gallup' where they returned to the original corridor which took them back to the UK.

While the first serials dropped paratroops near St Mére Eglise, the first serial of glider tugs had taken off from RAF Welford Park. This was the 434th TC Group, led by its CO Col William B. Whiteacre. Other glider tugs from the 437th TC Group followed. Over Normandy the combinations under heavy fire, were unable to maintain close formation and the units were scattered and intermingled on landing. Nevertheless, results of the landings differed more in detail than in mass, and the 101st Airborne Division was dropped without major loss, while only one unit of the 82nd Airborne Division was badly dropped. Despite the circumstances and some mistakes the airborne landings were a success, and aircraft losses were not high. Of the 821 troop carriers despatched, 805 reached their drop zones and 21 were lost. Of the 104 tugs and gliders, all but one reached the landing zone, and only two tugs were lost. The last paratroops were dropped at 04.04hr on 6 June.

The paratroops were resupplied between 20.53hr and 22.50hr in the evening of 6 June, and between 07.00hr and 08.55hr on 7 June by 408 tugs towing 408 Airspeed Horsa gliders in nine serials. The Waco CG-4A Hadrian gliders were used for night landings and the heavier Horsa for daylight. Further resupply was carried out on the morning of 7 June by 320 Douglas C-47s and C-53s. All things considered the airborne operations through the morning of 7 June when the last were flown, was a success. In total 1,662 aircraft and 512 gliders were despatched — 1,606 aircraft and 512 gliders crossed the English Channel and 1,581 aircraft completed their mission while 503 gliders were released at their landing zone. A total of 41 troop carrier aircraft was lost and 449 suffered from damage.

One view of the operations has come from Col Charles H. Young, commander of the 439th Troop Carrier Group:

'I was the Group Commander of the 439th Troop Carrier Group, based first at Balderton Field, near Newark-upon-Trent, then at Upottery, near Taunton, Somerset, for the Normandy operation. The lead airplane for our group was a C-47A 43-15159 coded D8-Z, which I named *The Argonia*, and used to lead our first mission into Normandy — 81 Douglas C-47s carrying paratroops of the 101st Airborne Division. Col Robert F. Sink, CO of the 506th Parachute Infantry Regiment, jumped from *The Argonia* into Normandy, and Lt-Col Melvin Zais, Battalion Commander of the 517th Parachute Infantry Regiment, had jumped out of it in Southern France. That same airplane was flown by our Group Operations Officer, Capt (later Lt-Col) Woodrow W. Smeck, to lead our second mission into Normandy with 50 airplanes towing 50 gliders (30 Horsas and 20 CG-4As). It was also used to lead our second mission into Southern France, towing CG-4A gliders.

'During the pilot briefings for the Normandy mission, which Col Robert F. Sink attended, I bet him five pounds that I could place him within

Above left: Douglas C-47A-40-DL 42-24051 c/n 9913 coded 'CN-N' from the 73rd Troop Carrier Squadron, 434th TC Group, drops supplies to the US troops trapped at Bastoigne in the winter of 1944. Personnel from 48 Air Despatch, Royal Army Service Corps were used in the drop to the 101st US Airborne Division who were surrounded. *IWM*

Above: Lt Pugh and Lt Wheeler from the 43rd Troop Carrier Squadron, 315th TC Group, discuss the flight from the UK at an airfield in France during 1944. The middle transport is *Mild & Bitter*. An aircraft from the 310th TC Squadron, 315th TCG is coming in to land. *IWM*

Below: Glider snatch was used in Europe and South East Asia Command. Depicted is a C-47 from the 91st Troop Carrier Squadron, 439th Troop Carrier Group, about to snatch off a USAAF Waco CG-4A Hadrian glider. The snatch gear on the C-47 plus the ground equipment is clearly visible. *IWM*

300yd of the spot he marked on his map of Drop Zone C and surrounding area, and I won the bet. He sent word back by one of his officers later that he had landed within 200yd of his mark, Of course some of our airplanes lost contact and scattered when we hit the cloud deck on the west coast of the peninsula, but we got a pretty good drop anyway. I was leading our formation using the auto-pilot, and never disengaged it nor changed course while we were in the clouds, although I slowly climbed above the cloud deck by moving the altitude control knob. After we got past the solid clouds, we made a gradual descent back to our briefed altitude and I left the auto-pilot on all the way to the DZ. On that same paratroop mission into Normandy, Major (later Lt-Col) Robert A. Barrere, CO of our 93rd TC Squadron was flying deputy lead on my right wing in C-47 42-100835 coded 3B. Lt-Col Chase of the 506th Parachute Infantry Regiment, 101st Airborne Division (who later became a Lt-General) jumped out of Barrere's airplane, and later wrote to him and told him we dropped him on the wrong side of the hedgerow in the centre of the DZ.

'The "D8" behind the cockpit on my airplane was the code for the 94th TC Squadron. Group Headquarters had no airplanes assigned to it, so pilots like myself in Group HQ drew our airplanes from the various squadrons of the group. The code for our 91st TC Squadron was L4; the 92nd J8, and the 93rd was 3B. We had several airplanes equipped with the SCR-717 radar with the tub antenna. I believe we had at least five so equipped, one for each of the Squadron Commanders and one for me. The tub antenna installation precluded the use of the para-racks under the belly. These airplanes were used as lead ships for our formations.

'On 17 September 1944, I flew The Argonia as

lead ship for our first mission carrying paratroops of the 82nd Airborne Division into Holland. The next day it was flown on a glider tow mission by our Group Liaison Officer, Capt Norman C. LaForest as back-up leader of our third mission into Holland, and he assumed the lead for the group when Maj Joseph A. Beck was shot down over Schouwen Island on the way in. Maj Beck was CO of the 94th TC Squadron, and with his crew was taken prisoner by the Germans but survived the war, except for Capt Fred O. Lorimer, his co-pilot, who was killed that day by German mortar fire after they crash landed.

'For our mission across the Rhine on 24 March 1945, The Argonia II was in second position, as Lt-Col Woodrow T. Merrill, CO of the 91st TC Squadron had never had a chance to lead a major mission and I let him lead this one, but I flew his wing up to the Rhine river where we split into two columns. I led the right-hand column to just north-east of Wesel to landing zone Z. The Argonia II was a new C-47B 43-48927, from the 91st TC Squadron, with "L4" on the fuselage behind the cockpit. It did not have the tub antenna.

'The 439th Troop Carrier Group, in addition to its four squadrons — 91st, 92nd, 93rd and 94th — had Group Headquarters, a Service Group, and for a time the 813th Air Evacuation Squadron. We participated in the Normandy, Southern France, Holland, Bastogne, Rhine, and many re-supply and evacuation operations. From Balderton, we moved to Upottery, then to Orbetello, Italy, then returned to Upottery. Briefly we moved to Rheims, France, back to Balderton, to Upottery again, to Alencon, then to Chateau-Verdun, France. Normally we had about 100 C-47s until after VE-Day, then changed to the Curtiss Commando or C-46, which we flew back to the USA in July 1945.'

Operation 'Varsity' was the airborne assault across the Rhine north and north-west of Wesel at 1000hr on 24 March 1945. The airborne units were flown to and dropped on their targets by 2,029 transport aircraft of the 9th Troop Carrier Command. The 50th, 52nd and 53rd Troop Carrier Wings operated from bases in France, leaving three groups — 315th, 316th and 61st — from the 52nd TC Wing, to operate from Boreham, Wethersfield and Chipping Ongar in the UK. Each wing had 81 Douglas transports on strength.

The first transports were over the target five minutes early, but all units were in good order and the formations excellent. After arriving over the target intense flak was encountered, and in the first 25 minutes nine transports were set on fire and six were shot down, all having dropped their paratroops. No aircraft were shot down by the Luftwaffe and most losses were due to anti-aircraft fire. 9th Troop Carrier Command lost a total of 46 transports in this final assault of World War 2.

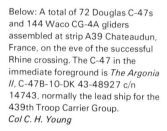

Below: A total of 72 Douglas C-47s and 144 Waco CG-4A gliders assembled at strip A39 Chateaudun, France, on the eve of the successful Rhine crossing. The C-47 in the immediate foreground is The Argonia II, C-47B-10-DK 43-48927 c/n 14743, normally the lead ship for the 439th Troop Carrier Group.
Col C. H. Young

In RAF Service

The Commonwealth air forces were much in evidence in the Middle East theatre of operations. Photo shows Royal Australian Air Force Personnel sorting out the vital rations just delivered by the RAF Dakota in the background from Sicily to this base on the Italian mainland where their RAAF fighter-bomber squadron was operating. *RAAF*

No 177 Wing ~ Operation 'Thursday'

Group Captain George F. K. Donaldson RAF (Retd)

No 177 (Airborne Forces) Wing was formed on 1 October 1943, at Rawalpindi, Punjab, India. Its function was to provide aircraft and aircrews to carry troops of the 50th (Indian) Parachute Brigade into battle in the South-East Asia theatre of war. The wing initially comprised three squadrons of Dakotas — Nos 62, 117 and 194. The nominal strength of aircraft in each squadron was 20, plus one or two reserves. The establishment of aircrews was about two per aircraft, a crew being made up of pilot, navigator, and two wireless operator/air gunners (Wop/AG), who were to add 'jumpmaster' to their qualifications. Squadrons were fortunate in having a strong Commonwealth element: picking a squadron at random, I found that, out of a total of 161 personnel, there were 20 from the RAAF, 22 from the RCAF, 5 from the RNZAF, and one from the SAAF. The 50th (Indian) Parachute Brigade comprised No 152 Indian Battalion, Nos 153 and No 154 Gurkha Battalions, plus Brigade Signals Section, and No 411 (Royal Bombay) Parachute Section, Indian Engineers.

The brigade had completed its basic training, and had been waiting for some time for operational parachutes, plus aircraft with which to train for battle. Priority was low, supplies going first to Europe and the Middle East. Eventually the C-in-C India, Gen Wavell, sent a personal signal to the Prime Minister, Winston Churchill:

'My Parachute Brigade has been starved of help and equipment from the UK, and much effort will be required if it is to play the very valuable part it might.' The signal yielded results. I met the Brigade Commander, Brig Tim Hope-Thompson, at the earliest opportunity. Battalion Commanders got together with squadron commanders, and a good liaison began to develop between our two formations. Apart from 62 Squadron, which had been based at Chaklala for several months, assisting No 3 Parachute Training School, the squadrons had little if any experience in paratroop dropping. They therefore underwent a short period of training, during which the Wop/AGs became 'jumpmasters', and pilots learnt the drill for dropping a stick of paratroops into a dropping zone (DZ). A 100% of the Wop/AGs, and most of the pilots and navigators also did the ground paratroop training course, followed by a 'live' jump. Most of the troops had done their basic training in old Vickers Valencia aircraft, dropping through a hole in the floor. These were replaced by Lockheed Hudsons which were not very suitable and only accommodated eight troops. The Douglas Dakota was therefore a great improvement, accommodating 20 fully equipped paratroops who ejected by stepping out of its wide doors.

Thereafter, operational exercises were discussed and planned, starting with a few aircraft, and working up to exercises involving the whole brigade, and the 60 odd Dakotas of 177 Wing. The aim was to reach a standard whereby the brigade could be dropped on a map reference point up to 400 miles distant, at a specified zero-hour. It required a plan on the 'count-down' principle, the most critical section being the time to be allowed for navigating and map-reading to the DZ, particularly at night, and perhaps by an indirect route. With our airborne force approaching readiness, we attended conferences at various Army HQ at which operations were discussed. At one of these, I recall, Lord Mountbatten took the chair. The use of the force in two operations in the Indaw area of North Burma looked promising. They were aimed at

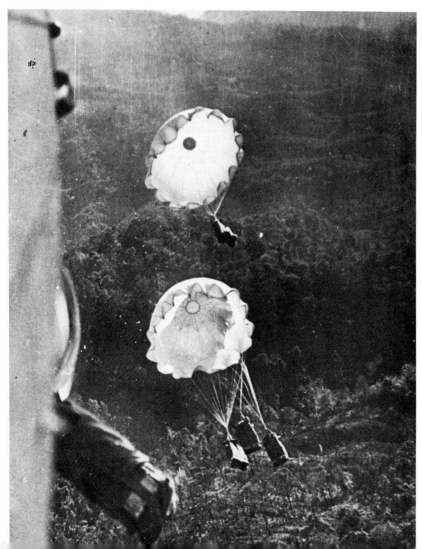

Below: A variety of vitally needed supplies being dropped from a 177 Wing Dakota to a DZ occupied by Orde Wingate's Chindits on patrol in the jungles of Burma somewhere behind the Japanese lines. The ideal height for dropping this type of parachute supply was between 600 and 700ft. *IWM*

assisting Gen 'Vinegar Joe' Stillwell and his Chinese forces. Alas, both had to be abandoned, owing, I think, to inability to obtain Gen Chiang Kai Chek's unconditional agreement. The most important operation would have been 'Bulldozer', a combined land-sea-air operation to recapture Akyab. But this also had to be abandoned, for various reasons.

It was now the beginning of 1944. The Japanese forces had advanced to the eastern frontier of India. If they defeated our army here, the road to Delhi would be open. All squadrons of the wing were ordered to the India Burma front. The 50th (Indian) Parachute Brigade, less one battalion, frustrated, also moved east to join in the conflict, not in their proper role as paratroops, but as light infantry. They were to play a gallant part in the forthcoming battle. After their long retreat through Burma, our forces were reorganising, and had started an advance in the Arakan. But they were meeting with formidable opposition from the Japanese, who had succeeded in cutting communications from the north. It had been planned from the start that the 81st West African Division, in the Kaladan River area in the east, would depend entirely on air supply. Now the remaining three Divisions — Nos 5, 7 and 26 — were virtually cut off, and Gen Bill Slim had called for all-out air-supply. Deciding the requirements of the army in the field and packing them ready for air supply, was the army's responsibility. The loading and the despatch of the packages from the aircraft was the responsibility of the RAF, though volunteer 'kickers out' from the army were always welcomed. The Dakota's maximum useful load was 7,500lb — $3\frac{3}{4}$ short tons — adjustable in relation to the fuel required for the flight. Parachute loads were ideally dropped from 600 to 700ft. Sometimes the nature of the terrain prevented aircraft going so low — often items which were not unduly affected by impact were usually dropped from about 100ft. Quite frequently parachutes failed to open. When this happened and the load was ammunition, the result could seem quite unfriendly. There was one case where a Dakota arrived back with petrol dripping from the fuselage. In his de-briefing the pilot said 'We found several of the cans were leaking, so we thought we'd better bring them back'. He must have been an Irishman. After dropping their load, aircraft would land at the nearest landing strip and pick up casualties. A typical report reads — 'Picked up 21 cases of smallpox, two of cholera, three died in plane.' The Arakan area was some 200 miles from base supply airfields at Comilla and Agartala. A sortie of this nature could take up to five hours. Quite often crews would fly two sorties in 24 hours. During February 1944, covering this phase, our aircraft dropped 3,955 tons, mostly by night to avoid enemy action. An extract from one of the squadron's operation record for 10 February reads. 'From 15.45hr on 10th, to 08.45hr on 11th, 19 aircraft flew 36 sorties. Our aim had been 47, but the Air Supply Section had been unable to keep up.' After their initial success in this sector; achieved by bold and aggressive tactics, the Japanese attack was

Below: Suitable sites for use as air strips had been noted during the first Chindit penetration behind the Jap lines, and these strips were prepared by engineers flown in by Waco CG-4A Hadrian gliders towed by Skytrains from 1 Air Commando. This is an aerial view of 'Piccadilly' and each jungle air strip was able to accommodate five or six Dakotas which flew in by day and night. *IWM*

55

repulsed. The troops of 15 Corps fought back with great spirit, and routed the Japanese army. Gen Slim wrote of it: 'The Arakan battle, judged by the forces engaged, was not of great magnitude. But it was, nevertheless, one of the historic successes of arms. It was the turning point of the Burma Campaign.' We were proud to have helped.

177 Wing HQ was now established at Agartala. On arrival we were augmented by 31 Squadron, which had already distinguished itself in supply dropping operations for Orde Wingate's first expedition into Burma. Nos 62, 117 and 194 Squadrons were dispersed at airfields in the vicinity, accommodated in hastily constructed 'bashas'. Conditions were primitive, but everyone remained cheerful and keen. Later we were reinforced by a detachment of 15 aircraft and crews from 216 Squadron in the Middle East, bringing our total strength to around 100 Dakota aircraft.

With the formation of a unified command in South East Asia, under Lord Mountbatten, a measure of integration between United States and British Forces was decreed. At our level it was decided that 177 Wing should integrate with four USAAF Douglas C-47 Skytrain squadrons, to form 3rd Troop Carrier Command. Brig-Gen William Old was to be Commander, and I was Deputy Commander. We were given offices in the same block as Gen Slim, commanding 14th Army, and Air Marshal Sir John Baldwin, AOC 3rd Tactical Air Force, under whom our new command came. It was a happy and workmanlike arrangement, enabling developments to be discussed and action initiated immediately. At squadron level, the integration made little if any impact. Gen 'Bill' Old was a keen and gallant pilot, who preferred to be flying than sitting at a desk. I don't remember ever getting a 'minute' from him — not even a 'loose' one. I see from my log-book that I flew 150hr 40min during February and March 1944, so there must have been times when both offices were vacant. We were fortunate in having a very good Senior Air Staff Officer (SASO) in 3rd TAF — Air Vice Marshal Gerald, later Sir Gerald, Gibbs, who did all the work.

Here I feel it would be helpful if I attempted a broad review of the military situation, so that the work of our squadrons may be put into perspective. As outlined earlier, No 4 Corps were now holding a front to the south, in the Arakan area, extending roughly from Kaladan westwards to the Bay of Bengal. From Kaladan the front ran generally north-east for some 700 miles to the Fort Hertz area, where Gen Stillwell held precarious sway with his Chinese forces. The intervening territory, poorly mapped, consisted largely of thick jungle, rugged mountain ranges, rivers and swamps; with many areas there for the taking by either side if they could negotiate the hazards. The mountain ranges and rivers ran north and south, thus forming a natural barrier between

Burma and India. To the west of this barrier the 14th Army was deployed with the main forces at Imphal, in a valley of that name, some 20 miles long by 10 miles wide, surrounded by mountains up to 8,000ft in height. Virtually the only supply route into the valley was from the railhead at Dimapur in the north, via Kohima, a distance of 130 miles, over a mountain range, across rivers, and through tortuous valleys.

Gen Slim realised that the primary objective of the Japanese must be the destruction of his Fourteenth Army. Faced with no simple options he decided (a) to withdraw his forces, deployed to the north and south, into the valley, and (b) to airlift the 5th Indian Division from the Arakan into the valley. Thus he hoped to achieve maximum concentration, and possibly numerical, superiority of his forces. Furthermore, he would be fighting on ground of his choosing, against an enemy whose communications would be extended.

But it was not to be quite as had been hoped. The Japanese probed west more rapidly and more fiercely than had been anticipated. To the south they cut off 17th Division's withdrawal route to the valley, making it entirely dependent on air supply. More seriously, to the north they cut the valley's only supply route from the railhead at Dimapur, at a point 30 miles north of Imphal. The date was 30 March 1944. On 5 April the 17th Division gallantly broke through the Japanese road block to the south, to join the beseiged forces in the valley. On 17 April Kohima, with its garrison of 3,000 was surrounded. Among the forces opposing the enemy around Imphal were our old friends, the 152nd and 153rd Battalions of the 50th (Indian) Parachute Brigade. At a place called Sanshak they were attacked by vastly superior numbers of the enemy. They held their ground despite a grave shortage of supplies, including water. Alas, many of our supply drops fell outside the DZ. However, the historian, K. C. Praval, in his book *India's Paratroopers* quotes this report by the commander of the 152nd Battalion:

'One aircraft however came very low and made a number of runs, so that we were able to collect the entire aircraft load. The pilot was magnificent. Each time he made his run, he was so low that the Japs opened up intense fire on him, while he waved and shouted encouragement. He was so low that we could see him waving to us, also the despatchers in the doorway. All subsequent supply drops were of the same pattern. On making enquiries afterwards, I learnt that the pilot and crew had taken part in the Brigade's air training at Chaklala. On hearing that the 50th Brigade was cut off, and having to rely entirely on air supply, they determined that whatever happened, and regardless of risk, the Brigade should get their entire load.'

Gen Slim wrote of this engagement. 'The ten days delay and the heavy casualties this small force, and the RAF who supported them, had inflicted on the enemy, were of inestimable value at this critical stage of the battle.' Despite this tribute, I have always regretted that aircraft of 177 Wing could not have done more to alleviate the desperate plight of our old colleagues.

Apart from 15th Corps, success in the Arakan, there had been little to cheer about in our struggle against the enemy. However, a man named Wingate had caught the imagination by a bold venture in which he marched a force into Japanese held Burma, disrupted enemy communications, skirmished with the enemy, and, battered but undaunted, marched out again. Now

Top left: Characteristic behaviour by a 'Recalcitrant Missouri' mule destined for Orde Wingates Chindits, as an attempt is made to persuade it aboard the 177 Wing Dakota transport. Often more than pure persuasion was required to get the mule up the ramp. The bamboo rails of the mule and pony stalls can be seen through the aircraft windows. *IWM*

Bottom left: Maj-Gen Orde Wingate confers with the CO of 1 Air Commando, Col Philip J. Cochrane (right) and his deputy Col John R. Allison (left) prior to Operation 'Thursday' which was launched on Sunday 5 March 1944. *IWM*

Above: Ghurkas and British West African troops waiting patiently to be flown into one of the airstrips behind the Japanese lines in US Troop Carrier Command Skytrains. The nearest one ('AB') is C-47A-70-DL 42-100686 c/n 19149. *IWM*

he wanted to repeat the operation. But this time he wanted his 3rd Indian Division to be flown in. The operation, to be code-named 'Thursday', was approved. The 177 Wing element of 3rd Troop Carrier Command was detailed to provide 40 Dakota and Skytrain aircraft to assist. The full and absorbing story of this unique operation has been well portrayed in other accounts. Here, I propose to confine myself to the part played by 177 Wing.

Briefly, the object of Operation 'Thursday' was to cut Japanese communications from the south, to their forces opposing Gen Stillwell and his Chinese forces in the north, so that the important task of building the Ledo Road to China, would not risk interruption. If Wingate's 3rd Indian Division, to be known as the 'Chindits' could be flown into strips strategically placed, time would be saved, troops would be fitter, and surprises more likely. Possible sites for strips had been noted during the first penetration. These strips were to be prepared by engineers flown in by gliders of Col Cochrane's US Air Commando. This was a legendary miniature air force, specially assigned by President Roosevelt for the sole use of Orde Wingate. As soon as the strips were ready, the Dakotas and C-47s of Troop Carrier Command would fly in the divisional troops and equipment.

The code names of the first two strips were 'Broadway' and 'Piccadilly'. On D-Day, 5 March 1944, 30 Douglas C-47s were lined up, each with two Waco CG-4A Hadrian gliders in tandem behind them, loaded with airfield engineers, troops, and equipment, including miniature bulldozers. Just before zero hour, a last minute photo-recce revealed that the area destined for 'Piccadilly' had been obstructed with large tree trunks. Despite the possibility that this might indicate that the Japanese had knowledge of the operation, and be waiting for us at 'Broadway', Gen Slim and Orde Wingate decided to continue, but switching the 'Piccadilly' contingent to 'Broadway'. As darkness fell at Hailakandi, the first C-47 Skytrain took off with its two gliders, followed at five minute intervals by successive aircraft. But trouble developed with the dual tow. Seventeen gliders broke away or had to release, to crash land, nine in hostile territory. The aircraft towing 11 gliders were recalled. But 32 gliders crash landed at 'Broadway'. Such were the landings — some gliders having no option but to crash into one another — that 33 were killed, and 30 seriously injured. The miniature bulldozers were lost. A few hours later, the codeword 'Soya Link' was received, meaning 'mission failed'. (For the uninitiated, a soya link was a horrible synthetic sausage.) We sent an aircraft over to drop more equipment. Then we received another signal which spelt out 'Pork Sausage' meaning 'OK'. Those who had survived, having piled up their dead, and succoured·the injured, got to work, often with their bare hands, and completed a magnificent job.

On the night of D+1 a total of 62 successful Dakota sorties were flown into 'Broadway', transporting troops, mules and equipment of 77 Brigade, commanded by Brig Mike Calvert, a part of III Brigade. On D+2 a second strip was prepared, code named 'Chowringhee'. Twenty-four aircraft were airborne for it when a message was received — 'Strip only 2,700 feet long'. Allowing for their full load, and trees at each end, this was a bit short, and a recall message was sent to all aircraft. However, seven aircraft 'did a Nelson' and landed — fortunately without damage. By D+5 the fly-in of III Brigade, commanded by Brig Joe Lentaigne, and certain other units, was completed.

For their role of harassing the enemy, the Chindits split up into columns, each Brigade comprising eight columns of 400 troops, plus mules and equipment. Two hours after the last column of III Brigade had left 'Chowringhee' the strip was bombed and strafed by Japanese aircraft. In addition to Hailakandi, our aircraft operated from strips at Lalaghat and Tullihall. The latter was a long strip but so dusty that, an aircraft taking-off raised a cloud of dust which delayed the next aircraft. There was little wind so we overcame this by positioning aircraft at the mid-way point, and taking-off alternatively in opposite directions. The transport of mules by air is worth a mention. These ubiquitous if temperamental creatures had long been essential to military operations in this kind of territory. Bamboo stalls for five mules were constructed in each Dakota with a straw-covered ramp lead up to the door. The muleteer would coax the mule up the ramp, and, with luck, into the stall. I was taking a load of mules into Chowringhee on D+2 when one refused to go up the ramp. Wingate was striding up and down in his somewhat impatient manner, and immediately came over. Taking the bridle from the muleteer, he proceeded to walk the mule around the aircraft showing it the various features. I understand that this is classic psychology — applied by the equine fraternity — akin to showing a horse a jump before hurtling it at the obstruction. I would like to report that it worked. But, alas, the mule took even greater exception — much to Orde Wingate's discomfort. Eventually it was manoeuvred in by six men and a rope. Some mules became very excitable in flight, and a number had to be shot before they kicked the side out of the aircraft. Nevertheless, they were valued so much, that when their tasks were done, we flew most of them out.

The animal establishment of a Chindit column, of which there were nine in each brigade, was nine ponies and 63 mules, and on the latter went the heavy equipment, such as mortars, flame-throwers, Piats, wireless sets, and medical and veterinary chests. By the end of March 1944, four of Wingate's Long Range Penetration brigades, each with some 650 animals, had been introduced into Burma by air. To fulfil their role of harassing the Jap lines of communications, columns had to

Left: Impressive air-to-air photo taken from C-47A-90-DL 43-15696 c/n 20162 from 1 Air Commando towing a Waco CG-4A Hadrian glider to an advanced airstrip in Burma. Gliders carrying airfield control equipment were normally the first to land on these strips behind the Jap lines. The communication cable between the tug and the glider can be seen along the tow-rope giving a frayed appearance. *Author's collection*

Above: Airstrip conference in full session during Operation 'Thursday' involving US personnel from 1 Air Commando, whose CO — Phil Cochrane — is in the centre. In the background is parked one of the 13 C-47s used by this unique unit in addition to a galaxy of other combat aircraft types. *Author's collection*

be highly mobile over all types of country, and for this mobility they depended more than anything on their mules, and in particular those which carried the all-important wireless sets. The possibility of paradropping mules was a very little publicised project carried out at the Air Transport Development Centre, Chaklala, Punjab, and trials were carried out using Dakota KG781. The mule was packed on to a platform which was fitted with two clusters of 28ft silk statichutes, dropped from the Dakota at 600ft flying 130mph. After several live drops, using young 900lb mules, 55min was allowed for packing from start to securing in the Dakota ready for take-off, and five to seven minutes on the DZ for releasing and saddling up. It was found that mules were capable of carrying a load within 15-20min of being dropped.

On the night of D+2, Air Marshal Sir John Baldwin came along and said, 'Have you got room for me, Donaldson?' Of course we made room — at the expense of my Canadian navigator, Olaf Meyer, who had to navigate standing up. Then Col Allison USAAF, who did a magnificent job sorting out the debacle at 'Broadway' on D-Day, appeared and said 'OK, if I join you fellers?' He squatted on the floor and promptly went to sleep within kicking distance of a mule. I was very touched by this gesture, which so naturally epitomised the solidarity and confidence which had developed between our American Allies and ourselves.

The jungle strips were shaped like the traditional thermometer, the bulb being the unloading area, able to accommodate five to six Dakotas. After unloading aircraft could only take-off in the opposite direction. We seem to have ignored winds. Flying Control was exercised by 'red' and 'green' with an Aldis lamp. By arrangement, we would split the night period between the USAAF squadrons and 177 Wing aircraft. On one

occasion we had the period up to 2330 hours. I was the last RAF Dakota off Broadway at about 2330. We were just starting our climb passing about 200ft when Olaf shouted — 'Aircraft dead ahead, Sir'. It passed directly over us with a dull roar, and our aircraft shook.

In a SITREP dated 9 March, Brig Tulloch, Wingate's Chief of Staff wrote, of Troop Carrier Command's part, ' — a marvel of efficiency and smooth working'. I had one reservation — during this first six-day phase, aircraft of 177 Wing transported into these jungle strips, 4,521 troops, 264 mules, 44 ponies, and 62,936lb of stores and equipment, and thereafter continued with supply dropping. One of the most unusual comforts dropped to the Chindits was Hesketh Pearson's book *Bernard Shaw*, indented for by Orde Wingate who had read a notice of Pearson's latest book in one of the newpapers sent in regularly by parachute. During the next supply drop the request was flashed to the circling Dakotas. A few days later the book, its pages still carrying the sharp, nostalgic tang of an English printing house, went hurtling down to the guerrilla leader's jungle HQ.

By D+2 the Chindits' 77 Brigade had established a stronghold which they christened 'White City', cutting the Japanese road and rail communications to the north. Thus they had carried out their first objective. On 25 March, in the second phase, 14 Brigade and the 3rd West African Brigade were flown into another strip, codenamed 'Aberdeen'. But on this same day we were shocked to hear that Gen Orde Wingate, the inspiration of this and its earlier unique operations, had been killed in an air accident. Brig Joe Lentaigne, the commander of III Brigade, was immediately appointed his successor. There followed the air supply of the Chindits as they moved through Japanese held territory, harassing the enemy. A further stronghold was established, codenamed 'Blackpool' at which reinforcements could be landed, and casualties evacuated. 'Blackpool' was attacked fiercely by the enemy. Anti-aircraft guns and medium artillery were brought up. Use of the strip became impossible, so supply had to be by dropping. On 25 May, the Chindits, carrying their wounded, broke out, evading the Japanese, to continue their task.

When I interrupted my review of the general situation to describe the Chindit operation, it was 7 April. Imphal was besieged; Kohima was also besieged. Thus our tasks were — air-supply of the Kohima garrison, the Chindits, our forces on the Arakan front, flying in reinforcements and supplies to Imphal, movement of personnel and equipment of RAF tactical squadrons to other airfields, the evacuation of casualties, and the collection and distribution of mail. The siege of Kohima was given priority by Gen Slim, because to have allowed it to fall without the stoutest resistance, would have made our supply base at Dimapur more vulnerable. So we engaged in an intensive supply dropping to the 3,000-strong gar-

rison there. The town was encroached upon by the enemy, until the garrison was confined in a space roughly 500yd square. All aircraft were having to run the gauntlet of ground fire, yet it is surprising that none was seriously damaged, though many were holed. I recall that we received a visit from an Armament officer from HQ in Delhi. He said he would like to accompany us on a sortie. I told him he could come with me as a despatcher. We had just completed our drop, when one of the regular despatchers popped his head into the cabin and said, 'Squadron Leader Paul's been hit, sir', 'Where, I replied', 'In his bum, sir.' Fortunately it was not serious, but he returned to Delhi somewhat chastened.

The seige of Imphal was probably the turning point of the war in South East Asia. In order to exist and fight, four Divisions of mixed British, Indian, and other nationalities, had to be supplied by air with all essentials. The operation was code named 'Stamina'. The Army's initial bid was for 400 tons per day to be flown in. Sir John Baldwin, in consultation with his staff, and Troop Carrier Command, accepted the bid. My recent researches of old records has brought home to me the expertise which the Army had developed in gauging and meeting the problems of supply. Here, for example, were the daily and weekly scales of rations for British and Indian troops. Some of the differences intrigued me. The bulk of Tommy's daily ration was 'Bread: 14oz' against the Sepoy's 'Rice 18oz'. Both were allowed $\frac{3}{4}$oz of salt. Tommy, $\frac{5}{8}$oz tea, and $3\frac{1}{2}$oz of sugar, against the Sepoy's $\frac{1}{3}$oz tea, and $2\frac{1}{2}$oz sugar. Tommy was allowed 50 cigarettes per week, as against 40 for the Sepoy. Both were allowed two boxes of matches unless you were a non-smoker, when you were allowed one. Tommy was rationed to 35 sheets of toilet paper per week; a Sepoy — none.

By this time the monsoon was developing, and the 8,000ft high mountains surrounding the valley

were frequently shrouded in thunderous cumulo-nimbus cloud and heavy rain. On many occasions it was impossible to fly into the valley. Khumbirgram was an airfield just to the west of the mountains — about 20min flying time away from Imphal. So it was decided that supplies should be stock-piled there awaiting clear weather, when all available Dakotas would concentrate on a rapid shuttle service. This arrangement was codenamed 'Hustle'. I recall being at Khumbirgram one day, and noticing a Dakota taking rather a lot of runway before getting airborne. A few minutes later it landed back. I went over in my jeep, to be met by the pilot, complaining that the aircraft would not climb. Just then a Flt/Sgt drove up, took one look through the fuselage door, and said, 'No . . . wonder; you've got a double load!' The aircraft had been carrying sacks of Ata (grain) a full load of which, weighing 7,000lb odd, would be three layers in depth. This aircraft had six layers. The maximum all-up weight of the Dakota at that time was 31,000lb. We reckoned that this one had taken off with about 37,000lb — and landed again safely. A great tribute to the Dakota.

Top: The scene at Lalaghat, Assam, on Sunday 5 March 1944, as the tow ropes from the Waco CG-4A Hadrian gliders parked in the background are stretched out ready to be hitched to C-47 glider tugs ready for Operation 'Thursday'. *USAF*

Above: Scene at Hailakandi airstrip in the Assam, India, during Operation 'Thursday' as an Air Commando C-47 Skytrain snatches a Waco CG-4A Hadrian glider off the ground. Glider snatch technique was developed for night operations by pilots of 1 Air Commando. *RAF Museum*

The siege of Imphal officially lasted from 18 April to 30 June 1944. During this period, in addition to other duties, aircraft of 177 Wing transported 4,399 tons of stores and equipment into the valley —and brought many casualties out. On 22 June, the vital road to Dimapur had been reopened, and Kohima had been relieved. By the end of June, Fourteenth Army was breaking out of Imphal on the offensive. After their heroic operations into enemy territory, most of the Chindits had been withdrawn or flown out for a well earned rest and recuperation. Those units remaining, merged into the Fourteenth Army's new offensive.

Third Troop Carrier Command was officially disbanded on 4 June 1944, and 177 Wing reverted to its earlier status. The role of the Wing remained the same, but we were now supporting an Army on the offensive. Although the diversity of our tasks might appear to have been reduced, in fact our work became more exacting and intensive. In their move eastwards and southwards, the Army were having to penetrate this mountainous, jungle covered terrain, which had from time immemorial formed an almost impenetrable barrier. Virtually all supplies had to be dropped. Dropping-zones were continually being moved, and were often difficult to find. The approaches to many were hazardous. Distances from supply bases were increasing. And overall, the monsoon was at its height. Nevertheless, in the ensuing months, squadrons increased their flying hours, one squadron taken at random, totalling 2,770 hours in June. This was a great tribute, not only to the aircrews, but to all our ground personnel who seldom allowed our aircraft availability to fall below 90%.

By September/October 1944, Fourteenth Army had cleared all pockets of enemy resistance around Imphal, and had advanced eastwards and southwards to a line roughly from Tamu in the north to Kalemyo in the south some 150 miles from Imphal. The Japanese had resisted fanatically all the way, as was evidenced by the massed bodies of dead found in villages overrun.

By now our squadrons were being relieved for rest and recuperation, which usually took the form of training at their old stamping ground in the Punjab. I was posted to 229 Group as Group Captain Operations towards the end of August, handing over command to Grp Capt C. N. Warrington. On 30 September 1944, 177 Wing was disbanded.

During its comparatively short existence, the Wing had trained for three to four months to carry a parachute brigade into battle — but without the satisfaction of doing so. Its role then changed to the support of the 14th Army and squadrons of the Third Tactical Air Forces, in virtually the whole range of their needs, from Bofors guns to butter, from mules, horses and oxen to toilet paper, from petrol and ammunition to drinking water, from motorcycles to jeeps, from tanks to Spitfires to aero engines, from battle trained troops to the evacuation of the sick and wounded. Of the last mentioned, Gen Slim wrote, 'Air evacuation did more in the 14th Army to save lives, than any other agency'. Our aircraft provided an air mail service which kept the troops in touch wherever they might be. An extract from the Operational Record of one of the squadrons reads; 12 May. Flg Off J. G. Simpson crashed "Clydeside" with 6,000 gallons of petrol and mail. Escaped, but went back to aircraft — now blazing, and rescued mail bags. This Dakota was Mk III FZ582 from 194 Squadron, known to all as 'The Friendly Firm'. In their eight months of operations on the Burma front, Dakotas from 177 Wing transported 36,102 tons of animals, stores and equipment, 31,217 troops, and evacuated 23,898 casualties. Fourteen aircraft were lost due to enemy action, nine due to weather, terrain and other causes, and many were damaged by enemy fire. A total of 61 aircrew was killed and four wounded. The relatively small scale of our losses was in large part due to the fighter escorts of Hawker Hurricanes and Supermarine Spitfires always available from the Third Tactical Air Force. Sometimes four, sometimes six aircraft would closely escort a sortie. We owed them a great deal.

The ubiquity of the Douglas Dakota in coping with its many tasks, and the conditions in which they were carried out, was only only matched by the ruggedness and simplicity. These qualities, together with the skill and dedication of our maintenance crews were paramount in the carrying of our job. Gallantry awards included 23 DFC's, one bar to the DFC, one BEM, and one DFM. Additionally our American Allies honoured us with six American DFC's.

War seems to be a necessary evil, leading inevitably to the destruction of human life. Few people can but abhor this aspect. It is perhaps some source of comfort that the operations of 177 Wing were in no small part directed to the sustaining of life, and the succour of the sick and wounded — tho' the cynic might well say, 'For What?'.

Below: Douglas C-47 Skytrain from 1 Air Commando seen en route from Palel, India to Meiktila, Burma with urgently needed troop reserves. Note the five white identification stripes round the transports fuselage, these being carried on most of the unit's aircraft. *USAF*

China~ Burma~ India

Left, top to bottom:

On 23 November 1941, A CNAC DC-3 No 47 arrived at Likiang near the Tibet border after the first flight over the 'Hump' on the commencement of a scheduled service from Hong Kong to Chungking, the provisional capital of China. The pilot on the epic flight was Capt Charles L. Sharp, and passengers included the CNAC Director, Arthur N. Young. *PAA*

For flying this USAAF C-47 Skytrain Maj L. Inparato won a DFC. Citation read, 'On 13 February 1943, a damaged C-47 was in need of a complete left wing to make it flyable. The spare wing was suspended beneath the fuselage of a second C-47 and despite danger of the wing tearing away or setting up vibration to wreck the aircraft or change its flying characteristics, he flew the wing 285 miles to an advanced area, where the damaged transport was repaired and flown out'. *USAF*

A good example showing the ruggedness of the 'Gooney Bird'. A Japanese suicide Kamikaze fighter-pilot attacked this C-47 Skytrain from the 1st Troop Carrier Squadron in Burma and when he failed to shoot it down, he tried to ram it, resulting in the damage shown in this photograph. There were many examples of damaged Skytrains and Dakotas making its safely back to base despite extensive battle damage. *Douglas*

Seen flying over typical 'Hump' terrain is C-47-DL 41-18456 c/n 4518 'J-Johnny' from an unidentified India-China squadron of Air Transport Command. The aircraft carries vital supplies across the 'Hump' route from India into China. According to the records this transport survived the war, only to be blown up in a bomb incident in Canada during 1949. *R. J. Soule*

63

Above: Appropriately named *Hap Gift* this C-47A-65-DL 41-100536 c/n 18999 was one of the personal transports used by the Supreme Commander, Lord Louis Mountbatten. It carries the Phoenix emblem of SEAC on the nose and retains its USAAF livery. The photographs were taken at Calcutta on 28 February 1945. The aircraft later served with the Thai Air Force.
P. M. Bowers

Centre right: Unusual livery on this C-47A-90-DL 43-15988 c/n 20454 of USAAF Air Transport Command seen at Agra, India on 1 August 1945. The aircraft still carries partial invasion stripes on the fuselage which indicate it was based in the UK during the time of the Normandy invasion on 6 June 1944.
P. M. Bowers

Bottom right: Whilst flying 'The Hump' or supply dropping the Dakota transports were always threatened by attack from Japanese fighters. This rare photo shows Vickers 'K' machine guns protruding from the Dakota window manned by crew members, whilst the fuselage is littered with an assortment of vital supplies waiting to be air dropped.
G. Vandervelt TIME-Life

The Friendly Firm

Flt Lt Douglas 'Chota' Williams

I was indeed most privileged to have been a founder member of 194 Squadron when the unit formed on 14 October 1942, at Lahore in the Punjab, near the Northwest frontier of India. The period I served with the squadron, from October 1942 to June 1944, was without doubt the most memorable and exciting time of my RAF service. The squadron 'sprang from the loins' of 31 Squadron, when Alec Pearson, Flight Commander, formed the nucleus of 194 Squadron from 31 Squadron personnel. The Air Ministry records reveal that local flying commenced on 15 October, and that nine days later the new CO, Wg Cdr Alex Pearson, took a Lockheed Hudson Mk VI to Dum Dum for stores with a crew of three. I had been crewed up in the UK with two Canadians — pilot Joe Curtis and navigator Jerry Walsh — a Scotsman, Jimmy Chapman, 2nd W/Op Air Gunner, and myself as W/Op Air Gunner with radar qualifications. We were based at Air HQ in New Delhi with the Comm Flight flying mail, freight and VIPs to various destinations in our Hudson. It was our good fortune to have as a passenger, on several occasions, Sqn Ldr 'Fatty' Pearson, then a flight commander with 31 Squadron, and when he formed his own squadron he invited us to join him. A Flight Commander was Sqn Ldr 'Turtle' Thirlwell and commander of B Flight was Sqn Ldr Frankie Bell.

In April 1943, 194 Squadron moved to Palam, Delhi, and continued the task of operating the airline routes with mail, freight and VIPs etc until later in the year when the unit handed over its commitments to 353 Squadron and we moved up to Basal in the Punjab for re-equipment with Dakotas. Fond as we were of the Hudson, we were still more than thrilled at converting to the Dakota, for we had now become 194 Airborne Forces Squadron, joining up with 62 and 117 Squadrons within the newly formed 117 Wing under Grp Capt George Donaldson based at Chaklala, Rawalpindi. The ubiquitous Dakota seemed to be the right machine for the job in hand, so we entered with great enthusiasm into the intensive operational training programme for the forthcoming invasion of Burma.

On 6 February 1944, two days after our last training exercise, 194 Squadron Dakotas led by 'Fatty' Pearson took off from Basal and headed for an unknown destination. The CO had his instructions in a sealed envelope, which for security reasons had to be opened in flight. The squadron formed up over Basal, having a beauti-ful view of the snowcapped Himalayas on our port side. After a long eight-hour flight we arrived at Comilla, Bengal, which was HQ Fourteenth Army. Rumours were rife on arrival, but after several hours we finally received word that we were to stay at Comilla to await further instructions. We spent three days and nights at this base, and we learnt later that this was due to the Japs pressing hard against the Indian 15th Corps in the Arakan, less than 100 miles away. The Japanese Fifteenth Army was facing our 4th Corps near the Imphal Plain, and one Jap Division, the crack 18th which had swept the Allied armies out of Burma a year before, now faced Gen Stilwell's Chinese divisions near Myitkina. The situation was critical with the Japanese aiming to advance, to capture Imphal and Kohima, preparatory to invading India in an all out offensive. All this action had the effect of delaying the movement of RAF squadrons in the forward areas. It turned out we had been waiting for 27 Squadron with its Beaufighters to move out of Agartala, our new base. Meanwhile various duties were allocated to 194 Squadron personnel, which included myself working shift duties in the Ops Room at Comilla, dealing with the daily operational strength of individual units available for sorties.

Below: Wing Commander Alec C. Pearson, CO of 194 Squadron, seen in the left-hand seat of a Douglas Dakota. 'Fatty' Pearson formed 'The Friendly Firm' at Lahore in the Punjab on 14 October 1942, initially equipped with the Lockheed Hudson. The co-pilot in the photo remains unidentified. *IWM*

Above: Dakota Mk III FD835 'G-George' (ex-C-47A-15-DL 42-23380 c/n 9242) of 194 Squadron seen on 24 March 1944, whilst helping to transport the 5th Indian Division from the Arakan to the Imphal Valley for the relief of beseiged Imphal and Kohima. A heavily loaded jeep is seen being loaded. *RAF Museum*

The squadron departed from Agartala on 9 February 1944, and no time was wasted for at midnight the same day our crew in Dakota 'H-Harry' was detailed to fly 6,000lb of supplies to the gallant Fourteenth Army in the Arakan. We arrived over the dropping zone at 01.45 and successfully delivered our load at Taung Bazaar after a ground signal clearance. We arrived back at base at 03.30 for a most welcome breakfast and a kip. Later that day we received orders for a further sortie to Taung Bazaar.

After a day and a half of rest, we were detailed to take 'C-Charlie' back to the Arakan, taking off at 21.05 on 12 February. On arrival at the DZ we were very surprised to encounter anti-aircraft fire. We circled twice, the firing continued and it became obvious that the area was in Jap hands. So we set course for home. On looking back out of the rear loading door I suddenly spotted what appeared to be a fighter silhouetted against the dark sky. I called Jimmy Howe, my fellow w/op to have a look, and he confirmed my fears. I dashed up to the cockpit and shouted to our pilot, Joe Curtis, 'Bandits, evasive action, quick'. Joe acted immediately, corkscrewing the aircraft, and we returned to base undamaged, considering ourselves very lucky. It was a relief to be allocated a day sortie two days later!

For this mission we took off at 14.40, arriving over the DZ in the Arakan at 16.30. We did a normal run to identify ourselves to the allied troops, when we spotted huge puffs of smoke in the jungle and fields below which indicated the battle was still in progress. We commenced our supply drop at 500ft and had to pass over enemy lines on each circuit. On one of the runs we actually heard gunfire over the roar of the Twin Wasp engines. Suddenly black smoke rushed past

the loading doors as Jimmy Howe and Ian Darnley stood with me steadying the bales on the static line ready for the next drop. I rushed up to the cockpit as the Dakota lurched, to be told by Joe that the port engine had been hit and that he had feathered the props. I was instructed to warn the rest of the crew in the rear, and to prepare ourselves in case of a crash landing. There was still quite a load of supplies on board, and it was evident that Joe was having difficulty in maintaining height on one engine. We were now very low, and I thought a crash landing was inevitable, and wondered in whose territory it would be. I need not have worried, as Joe was a strong and capable pilot. He held the transport steady. Our competent navigator, Ian Darnley, gave him a course to steer for base and we headed for home. We soon got rid of the remaining supplies, and often wondered who got them. We were the first 194 Squadron crew to be hit by Jap ground fire during a supply drop. We learnt later that a Hawker Hurricane pilot who had been providing air cover over the area, had reported us disappearing in a cloud of black smoke, believed crashed. But Joe Curtis with magnificent skill and encouragement from the crew, managed to gain height sufficiently to lift 'C-Charlie' over the Chin Hills on the starboard engine. As we neared base I made a radio call to alert the station ambulance and crash crews for an emergency landing. It was fortunate for us that 194 Squadron's first blooding in battle ended safely. After a return flight of nearly two hours on one engine, we homed in to the welcome sound of Agartala beacon, and made a perfect landing. Our two fitters, Ken Moses and Frank Bishenden gave us a rousing welcome as we arrived in dispersal. Counting our blessings later in the mess over several bottles of Scotch, we

Left: Dakota Mk III FL513 (ex-C-47A-50-DL 42-24169 c/n 10031) from 194 Squadron with a mule being persuaded into the transport! This Dakota, piloted by Grp Capt George Donaldson, took Air Marshal Sir John Baldwin into the 'Broadway' strip during the first night of Operation 'Thursday' in March 1944. *IWM*

were greatly saddened by the news that Joe Curtis had been reprimanded for not landing the crippled transport at the nearest satellite strip on the way home.

After only five days of battle action we were fast becoming campaign veterans, and only nine days after the squadron had moved from Basal over 1,000 miles away. The Japanese commander, Tanahashi, had struck a severe blow against our 15th Corps in the Arakan and the 7th Division was surrounded. The supply by air of arms, ammunition and rations was now crucial to their survival. Flying supplies down the Ngakyedauk Pass was a hazardous task, for Jap fighters had not been completely cleared from the skies over Burma by our fighters. In an all out effort to support the beleaguered troops, USAAF Troop Carrier Command and RAF Dakota squadrons, which included 194, were now flying a shuttle service of daylight sorties along both sides of the Mayu Range supported by fighter cover.

On 16 February our crew were back in the saddle using Dakota 'G-George' fully laden with 7,000lb of supplies. We flew in vic formation of three transports supported by a fighter escort of six Hurricanes. By the following day our hard working ground staff had restored to service our beloved 'C-Charlie' and over the next 11 days continued supply dropping missions down the Arakan with occasional sorties to the garrison at Tiddim, in the Chin Hills, enjoying a comforting escort of eight Hurricanes on most trips. All sorties were successful. There had been some bitter and fierce battles around the Buthidaung and Maungdaw tunnels, but with the massive supply drops from the Dakotas, Bill Slim's Fourteenth Army was now getting the upper hand over the fanatically brave Japanese in the

Arakan, a situation which later enabled the 5th Indian Division to be flown out to help the besieged Imphal.

Dakota 'C-Charlie' was flown to Lalaghat on 27 February along with other squadron crews for a glider-towing exercise returning to Agartala late that evening. The following day we flew down to Chandina to assist the USAAF on supply sorties in the Kaladan Valley. Flying records were already being broken and 194 Squadron flew approximately 1,500hr in just under three weeks. This fine achievement, plus the excellent performances of other Dakota transport squadrons, helped change the course of the Burma campaign in favour of the Allies.

On 4 March 1944, 13 Dakotas from 194 Squadron were detached to Tulihal in the Imphal Valley, to participate in Operation 'Thursday' the air invasion of Burma which involved flying troops, equipment, mules, ammunition and food,

Above: Dakota Mk III FL578 (ex-C-47A-1-DK) seen loading heavy guns for Imphal on 24 March, 1944 during the airlift of the 5th Indian Division. Pilot was Sqn Ldr Frankie Bell, Navigator Flg Off Ken Hale and w/op Flg Off Norman King, all from 'The Friendly Firm'. *RAF Museum*

Above: Carrying the 'Flying Elephant' insignia of 194 Squadron, two Dakotas from 'The Friendly Firm' are seen parked somewhere in Burma after unloading Ghurka troops. The air and ground crew are seen conferring on the left of the photograph. *IWM*

one battlefield to another, hundreds of miles apart. My crew in faithful 'C-Charlie' did three sorties on the first day with our first at 06.20 down to Dohazari in the Arakan, carrying men, mules and equipment up to Imphal. This operation continued for three more days, and included the evacuation of casualties. Meanwhile our old friends of the 50th Parachute Brigade, with whom we had trained at Basal, had moved to Ukhrul fighting as infantry, inflicting heavy losses on the invaders and holding them in check for several days.

The Japanese reached the hills overlooking Imphal airfield north of the town, but the 5th Indian Division fresh from their airlift and now reinforced with tanks, dislodged the enemy and prevented their guns from doing any serious damage. Mountbatten's action had been justified as neither Kohima nor Imphal fell to the enemy. On 24 March we flew our last two trips transporting the 5th Indian Division, transporting men and guns from Agartala to Imphal and airlifting 11 Squadron out of Imphal to Pathalkandi.

By now Brig Bernard Ferguson had established another Chindit stronghold at a rough strip behind enemy lines codenamed 'Aberdeen' which Wingate had named after his wife's home town. The Friendly Firm was called upon to fly-in reinforcements, men, mules and equipment from Lalaghat in the Assam Valley. My crew in 'C-Charlie' did 12 sorties into 'Aberdeen' logging both day and night time, sometimes in vic formation of three Daks with fighter escorts of six Hurricanes and top cover of up to 20 Spitfires.

The strip at 'Aberdeen' was eventually evacuated on 2 May 1944, when the last aircraft took off and the Chindits departed. They left behind the wreckage of between 20 and 30 Dakotas which had been badly damaged either landing or taking-off from this primitive strip.

At 07.05 on 9 April we were airborne again for Palel — the all-weather airstrip on the Imphal Valley, which the Japs were keen to capture. We flew via Silchar with a load of bombs. At Palel we were to assist in the airlift of a Hurricane squadron as Jap artillery was dominating the runway. We loaded 'C-Charlie' with 22 personnel and equipment whilst the Hurricanes bombed and strafed the enemy in the surrounding hills. We proceeded on a normal take-off, when, at the point of becoming airborne we encountered a terrifying gusty cross wind which suddenly blew across the valley. As one wing dipped dangerously our pilot, Joe Curtis, with great presence of mind thumped the throttles back, injuring his wrist. He abandoned take-off and with great skill managed to level the Dak as we bounced heavily back on the runway. The oleo legs collapsed, as I think we hit a ditch, and I opened the door leading from the wireless cabin and called to the passengers to disembark calmly. We all sat on the ground, pretty dazed. Joe Curtis, Ian Darnley, Jimmy Howe and myself were greatly upset at the state of our beloved

into improvised airstrips nearly 200 miles behind enemy lines.

By 11 March the main part of Operation 'Thursday' was complete. A great deal of its success was due to the Spitfires from 221 and 224 Groups keeping at bay the Jap reconnaissance flights, plus the USAAF P-51 Mustangs with 1,000lb bombs who attacked the Jap fighter bases at low level. Not one Dakota was lost, although one or two from the squadron were damaged either in landing or taxying incidents, but they were repaired on the spot by Flt Sgt Ken Aiken with his crew of riggers and were able to be flown out.

We left Tulhihal and returned to Agartala and over the next seven days our Daks were active on normal supply dropping sorties to the Chindits and Fourteenth Army. On 20 March 15 transports were switched to the Arakan to help transport the 5th Indian Division, lock, stock and barrel, including mules and heavy guns, up to the Imphal Plain to reinforce besieged Imphal. Bill Slim had by now mastered the Japs in the Arakan, but the situation at Imphal and Kohima had become critical. The Japs had dug themselves in along the Tiddim-Imphal road and were rapidly building up their forces along this front for a thrust into India, boasting in their propaganda broadcasts that they would be in Delhi by Christmas. To assist in airlifting the 5th Indian Division, Mountbatten ordered 24 C-47s off the Hump route to China. This was the first ever transportation by air of a complete division from

Left: West African troops board a 194 Squadron Dakota 'E-Easy' for a reinforcement flight to Imphal during March 1944. At this period the Daks and crews were operating night and day dropping supplies behind the Jap lines, supply dropping in the Arakan, and evacuating sick and wounded from forward areas. *IWM*

Below: After VJ-Day the task of the RAF transport squadrons in South East Asia Command was to bring back the many PoWs including many civilians. Photo depicts a 194 Squadron Dakota, one of many, with its load of passengers whose faҫial expressions speak for themselves. *IWM*

'C-Charlie' which was a write-off. It was a Dak which had served us wonderfully well on most of the operational sorties into Burma. It was just like losing a home, for we had worked many hours on board her, and so many periods of 40 winks beneath her wings between ops — we suddenly felt insecure and lost. Things were never the same after this fateful episode.

We carried on flying other transports as and when available. During May landings were made at yet another new Chindit airstrip in Burma called 'Clydeside' — a murderous spot full of shell holes, and I would have said much worse than 'Aberdeen'. On 12 May 'Clydeside' claimed a 194 Squadron victim. Joe Simpson with his crew, 'Robbie' Robinson, John Carr-Lawton and Southwood, were in Dakota FZ582 when it broke its port undercarriage leg on landing. The unharmed crew had barely got out of the aircraft when it caught fire. The cargo was petrol and mail bags. Joe remembered the Chindits' mail and at great personal risk climbed back on board the blazing fuselage to rescue the precious bags.

Early in June 1944 the Squadron was deeply involved in the important action of relieving Kohima. Deryck Groocock was called upon to take part in a large scale supply drop, and he relates one of the most amazing stories of monsoon flying:

'The DZ was in a valley north of Kohima. Twelve aircraft were sent there independently. The whole of the area was covered with a 10/10ths layer of cloud, which prevented us from seeing the ground. The tops of the Chin Hills in this area were about 7,500ft. The 194 Daks were flying at 9,000ft, just above the layer of smooth, grey cloud. We hoped to find a hole in the cloud which would enable us to let down below cloud near the DZ and then find it. As we neared our ETA, the two w/ops, Harvey Bell and Chuck Atherton, went to the back of the aircraft to organise the load of rice bags for a free fall drop. This was when things began to go wrong. I noticed the speed of the aircraft began dropping. My natural reaction was to put on more power, which I did. However, the speed continued to drop off and, up front, we started to get really worried. I did not appreciate at first what had happened, that the movement of rice sacks to the rear of the Dakota, which itself had probably not been properly loaded — there were no trim sheets in those days — had almost certainly put the centre of gravity beyond the safety limit. Anyway, the airspeed was getting alarmingly low, but I was unable to push the nose down to gain speed, because of the lack of height between us and the mountain tops. Suddenly the Dakota flickered over to port and went into a spin, taking us through cloud and we could see nothing. Watching that altimeter spin round and waiting for the crash into the mountains, I took the normal spin recovery procedure — stick forward and opposite the rudder. I think by now the sacks of rice near the door had fallen forward, because after agonising seconds watching the altimeter spin round down to 4,700ft we suddenly broke cloud under control and found ourselves in a green valley, between two ranges of hills which vanished up into clouds. After this miraculous escape we flew up the valley, a very shaken crew, then dead ahead of us, we spotted a column of smoke. We continued to fly towards it and to our amazement, we made out an Army DZ party and the markings of the very dropping zone we had set out to locate. We waved madly at the chaps on the ground and flew round until we had got rid of those flaming sacks of rice. Our next job was to get out of the valley and above the clouds without hitting the hills. We could find no way out under the cloud, so we just had to find the centre of the widest point of the valley and climb up through cloud in a steep climbing turn, praying the wind would not blow us in the wrong direction. After a few tense minutes we popped up safely through the cloud again and returned to base. When we landed we learned that we were the only crew to have successfully made a drop that day.'

The squadron subsequently received a signal of congratulations from the Army column commander, and Deryck said, 'Little did he know how he came to get his rations for that day'.

During the period March to July, 1944, 194 Squadron averaged over 2,000 hours monthly, mainly in support of the Chindits and in supplying the besieged garrisons at Imphal and Kohima. The squadron received many commendations from Army sources for their part in these operations, and its motto 'The Friendly Firm' adopted by 'Fatty' Pearson when he formed the squadron in 1942 from a motor transport company of that name in Lahore, was now well known throughout India and Burma. Because of the winged 'Dumbo' painted on the transports, both Hudsons and Daks, unit was nicknamed 'The Flying Elephants' and affectionately remembered by Wingate's Chindits and Fourteenth Army. In recognition of 194 Squadron's achievements the CO 'Fatty' Pearson, and the two flight commanders, Frankie Bell and 'Turtle' Thirlwell, were awarded the DFC. The CO had previously been awarded the American DFC. He had earned a new appointment and to everyone's dismay was posted from the squadron. He was presented with a silver plate engraved with the signature of every officer on the squadron in recognition of his great popularity. Wd Cdr Robert Chisholm of 117 Squadron assumed command.

Other changes of personnel were also taking place. Canadian crews from the two RCAF squadrons were being repatriated home. A number of pilots were posted out to 9 Ferry Unit and 1334 Transport Support Training Unit at Chaklala. Jimmy Howe and myself were posted to Chaklala as Signals Instructors (Air) to be joined by navigator 'Flash' Beaumont as unit adjutant. We had all done well over 90 sorties into Burma, including over 20 landings behind enemy lines, as had most crews on the squadron. The month of July 1944, saw many changes, but veterans like Eric Woodiwiss, Ken Edwards, Charlie Furman and Bill Coysh stayed with the squadron as did the Adjutant Andy 'Windsock' Chalmers and Doc 'Tarmac' Turnbull who vied with each other to get more hours recorded in their respective log books and impressive totals they were for ground wallahs. Morale on 194 Squadron was very good and the great spirit of 'The Friendly Firm' which had been inspired by its founder 'Fatty' Pearson lived on. It was to be 15 February 1946 before the squadron was disbanded.

Right: On 31 January 1945, the Flying Elephant badge was submitted to Chester Herald for approval, but was described as unsuitable by higher authority. However the Flying Elephant insignia was proudly carried by 'The Friendly Firm' on its Hudson transports and later its Douglas transports including the ubiquitous Dakota. *Author's collection*

In the Middle East

Left: Takoradi was a huge British air base built out of the red clay of the Gold Coast in June 1940 and in operation just three months later. This photo was taken later in World War 2 and shows two Douglas Dakota transports, an Avro Anson, plus a Vickers Armstrong Wellington bomber, all parked on the huge dispersal area. *IWM*

Below: This C-47-DL, 41-18529 c/n 4621, was operated by the RAF in the Middle East and is seen on 22 December 1943, unloading casualties into US ambulances. This aircraft was assigned to Africa in December 1942 after its completion at Long Beach. *IWM*

Above: Dakota Mk III FD857 S-Sugar
from 267 Squadron
(ex-C-47A-20-DL 42-23463 c/n
9325) flying over the picturesque
Grecian islands near Missolonghi on
the way back to its base at Araxos
airstrip in Greece during October
1944. *Author's collection*

Right: Camouflaged Dakotas of 267
Squadron parked at Bari, Italy during
1944. Dakotas Mk III KG496, FL586
and FD857 are in the foreground.
Other types identified in the photo
include Thunderbolts, Lightnings,
Liberators, Fortresses and many more
ubiquitous Dakotas.
Author's collection

Below right: Ancient and modern
modes of transport are united at a
partisan airstrip in Greece during
September 1944. The two parked
Dakotas are from 267 Squadron, a
Middle East transport unit heavily
involved in a wide variety of task s
and operations. *Author's collection*

The Flying Nightingales

Throughout the months of 1943 there had been much argument and discussion over the arrangements for the evacuation of casualties, and it was not until 22 May 1944, that a definite policy was agreed upon, as a result of a War Office conference. It was decided that six Handley Page Harrows, renamed Sparrows, from 271 Squadron and 70 Avro Ansons from Flying Training Command, were to be available for use in forward areas for casualty evacuation. A casualty rate of 600 per day by D+40 was allowed for and these were to be accepted at 200 per day at the airfields located at RAF Broadwell, Lechlade, Gloucestershire; Blakehill Farm, and Down Ampney, Cirencester, Gloucestershire. A control HQ was set up at Swindon in direct contact with the airfields, hospitals and ambulance units. No 46 Group completed its first task of casualty evacuation one week after D-Day, when Dakotas flew 23 Army and one RAF casualty from France to RAF Blakehill Farm. By 28 July 1944, 10,000 casualties had been transported back to the UK. The Ansons detailed from Flying Training Command for use in cases of emergency were modified to carry either freight or casualties. A reserve pool of 50 aircraft was stationed at RAF Watchfield, near Swindon, but they were scarely ever used.

By the end of November 1944, over 47,000 sick and wounded from the Western Front in Europe, had been flown to hospitals in the UK by aircraft of RAF Transport Command. Over 98% of these were British and Dominions Army personnel. Every one of them was in the care of the RAF Medical Branch from the time they entered the aircraft, usually a Dakota, on a landing strip in Europe, until they were distributed to Army medical establishments and hospitals in the UK by a RAF Casualty Air Evacuation Centre or, in some cases, by a RAF Casualty Clearing Station after reception from the CAEC the vast majority of Army casualties came in contact with the RAF Medical Branch for the first time when they were evacuated by air. Troops fighting on the Second Front who became casualties, whether through enemy action or sickness, and who were unlikely to be fit within a month, entered a channel of evacuation which ended at hospital in the UK. There were four ways in a combination which enabled a casualty to reach the home-based hospital: road, rail, sea and air. The quickest combination naturally was by road and air. For example of two casualties, one could be flown to the UK and be in a hospital in Southern Endland in seven hours; whilst the other could be put on an ambulance train, and later join an aircraft, but 12 hours was nothing to cover a 60-odd mile journey by train on a single-track.

When a man was wounded in action, it was certain that the knowledge that he was to be evacuated to a home-based hospital made him look forward to something more comfortable and personal in the way of attention. Naturally the mind projected forward to thoughts of 'home'. Although the types of casualty carried in any one Dakota fluctuated considerably, an average taken at one Casualty Air Evacuation Centre over a

Left: The first three operational WAAF nursing orderlies selected to fly in Dakota aircraft, to recover casualties from Normandy. Left to right: LACW Myra Roberts; Cpl Lydia Alford; and LACW Edna Birbeck. They are seen here in their operational flying gear, prior to take-off. *E. Morris*

period of a month showed that two-thirds of the casualties flown home were injured between two and five days previously, and one-sixth were injured less than 24-hours previously. The remainder were cases with more than five days' history. Two-thirds of the total number of cases were limb-injuries. This meant that of an average number of cases carried in one aircraft-load, the vast majority were fully sensitive to their surroundings, and certainly retained impressions of the journey home and the treatment they received. Judging by results, air evacuation made two important contributions towards the recovery of casualties. When the number of casualties with special injuries exceeded the number that could be accommodated by neuro-surgical and other specialised units in the field, it assured the surplus numbers of equal treatment of flying them in time to home units where they received the attention required. Some cases of head injury were received here in the UK less than eight hours after injury. The second contribution applied to the majority of casualties — those who were able to take notice and who had never flown before. For these, the fact of air travel alone provided an astonishing stimulus to morale. If there was a WAAF nursing orderly, and not an airman, in attendance — there was

Above: The first wounded to be brought back from Normandy by air were transported by Dakota transports on D+7 — Friday, 13 June 1944. LACW Edna Birbeck checks her patients consisting of 23 Army and one RAF casualty. Three Dakotas were used with a WAAF nursing orderly on each transport.
Fox Photos

Right: A nursing sister of the Princess Mary Royal Air Force Nursing Service assisted by WAAF nursing orderlies, receives a casualty transported by a Dakota at a Casualty Air Evacuation Centre somewhere in the UK during 1944. *MoD*

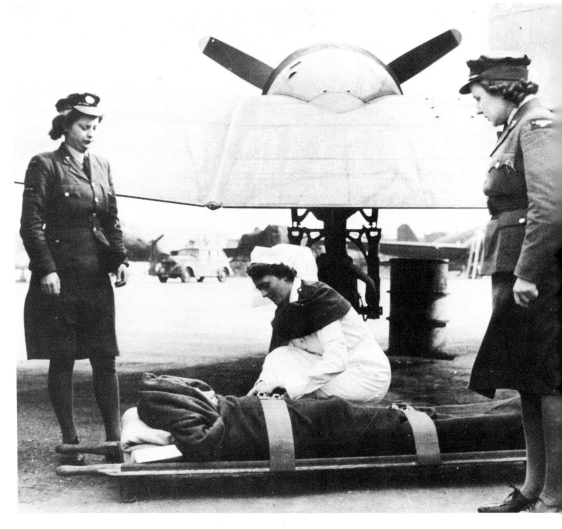

always great delight at the sound of a girl's voice talking in English. Certain reactions and concern by a patient occurred so often, that they could easily be tabulated. 'Where are we going, which way, how long, and will I end up near home?' 'Tell me the moment we are over the coast of England' 'What is it going to be like when we take off, and when we land?' For those anticipating something unusual, both take-off and the landing proved to be disappointingly dull — and some said so. Lulled by the background noise of the Dakota engines, many fell asleep — encouraged by the fact that home lay ahead, they had been made comfortable by the WAAF nursing orderly, or airman, and had been given the life-saving cup of tea and a cigarette.

For the nursing orderly, the amount of responsibility in attending to 18 lying and six sitting patients in any one Dakota load was subject to variation. During lulls on the battlefront, or when only local engagements took place, the workload was lighter than when heavy battle attacks were in progress. Then the number of cases wounded less than 48 hours previously rose in proportion to the pressure exerted on medical units in the field. The battles in the Caen area, Falaise Gap and Arnhem, are particular examples. The greatest call on an orderly's resource and skill were made most frequently by cases of head injury who needed pacification; tracheotomies, colostomies and facio-maxillary cases who needed very careful and sustained attention; plus chest cases who, in addition to attention, required oxygen. Cases of air sickness were the exception and not the rule. Generally

speaking, the nursing orderly worked hardest during the first hour of flight, after which some of the cases had settled down to sleep, whilst the rest were happily anticipating the reception that awaited them at the other end of the journey in the UK.

The Casualty Air Evacuation Centre was a RAF medical unit specially designed to receive, treat, sustain, and sort casualties at the end of their journey by air. The ones in the UK had an added responsibility in that it was here that the casualty received his very first welcome to his home country in whose cause he had been fighting hundreds of miles away, perhaps up to his waist in water, or cramped in the heat of a tank in battle, or in some other circumstance equally demanding fortitude and endurance. In the case of Dominions personnel, the expectancy of a welcome was not altered.

The national daily newspapers here in the UK revealed for the first time on Saturday 14 June 1944, eight days after D-Day, that RAF Dakota transports with WAAF nursing orderlies were being used to bring back casualties from the invasion front in France. The first flight, according to the newspapers, was an experiment and the extent to which air evacuation of wounded replacing evacuation by sea largely depended on a verdict by the Air Ministry. However arrangements had already been made for extensive air evacuation. The first three WAAF nursing orderlies were Corporal Lydia Alford, of Eastleigh, Hants; Leading Aircraft Woman Myra Roberts, of Oswestry, Shropshire; and Leading Aircraft Woman Edna Birbeck, of Wellingborough,

Above: Dakota FZ607 (ex-C-47A-1-DK 42-92370 c/n 12162) off-loads casualties at a UK airfield. Note the D-Day invasion stripes obscuring most of the serial number, and the pierced-steel-planking on which the Dakota transports are parked. This Dak survived the war and was sold as surplus to requirements. *IWM*

75

Above: Dakota FZ622
(ex-C-47A-1-DK 42-92383 c/n
12177) named *Kwicherbichin UK*
from 233 Squadron, returning from
Normandy on 1 August 1944, with
wounded. Aircrew from the
Commonwealth were integrated into
RAF Transport Command crews. This
Dak also survived the war, and went
to BOAC. *RAAF*

Northants. Edna Birbeck recalls her experiences:
'We were attached to 233 Squadron based at
RAF Blakehill Farm, near Cricklade, joining the
unit at the end of March 1944. My first flight in a
Dakota was on 20 April which was a training
flight for the crew, and the aircraft was without its
cargo doors. I was feeling sick so left the cabin for
the "little room" at the rear. The W/Op realised I
had gone and was terrified, thinking I had fallen
out. All was well when I appeared looking slightly
green. The W/Op was Glyn "Taffy" Morris who
I eventually married. Another nurse married the
navigator from the same 233 Squadron Dakota
crew, both on 31 March 1945.

'Prior to D-Day I did a refresher course at
RAF Wroughton hospital. At RAF Blakehill
Farm there was a large field hospital — a
Casualty Air Evacuation Centre — under
canvas, during the early days after the Normandy
landings, but later all casualties were moved out
by ambulance after arrival by Dakota. Later we
landed casualties at CAEC's located at both
RAF Down Ampney and Broadwell. I personally
escorted by air a total of 630 casualties from the
war front, including 526 stretcher and 104 sitting
cases. The bases flown to in Europe were
numerous.

'Our first operational sortie took place on
Friday 13 June 1944, the three nurses chosen for
the task were confined to Sick Quarters the night
before, with only a vague idea of what was
happening. At dawn on the day, after an aircrew
breakfast, we were taken out to our three
Dakotas. The crew of our Dak were Australian
— Flg Off Hamilton and Sgt Jimmy Firth W/Op
who were all later killed at Arnhem — we had an
escort of Spitfires as we crossed the Channel, and
as we approached the French coast the sea
appeared to be full of small boats. The landing
was on a metal strip runway laid down in a field

of corn with poppies still in bloom around the
edges, but it was like a sandstorm when the
Dakota landed and we were all soon smothered in
yellow dust. The aircraft was quickly loaded with
wounded, but was unloaded later from two of
them. One Dakota took off before the weather
closed in, and we had a wait of several hours,
during which time we were taken on a tour of the
local villages by a war correspondent. Snipers
were still around and we could hear the barrage of
guns and bursting bombs, and saw one aircraft
shot down. A column of marching troops on their
way to the battle front passed us, and cheered us
on our way, one with eyes popping remarked
"Blimey, women". Eventually we re-loaded and
took off with ten stretcher cases on board — the
first evacuation of wounded from France by air
had been successfully completed. Later I received
a letter of congratulations from the AOC (Air
Officer Commanding) addressed to Corporal
Birkbeck, so I naturally thought I had been pro-
moted, but it was a slip of the pen of officialdom.

'The flights to the Continent were approved by
the Air Ministry and soon operated on a regular
basis. We nurses carried large flasks of tea with
us on the aircraft, which was most acceptable by
the wounded. We also had our pannier of medical
supplies. The initial flights to France were all to
emergency airfields, lacking any facilities, but
later as the front progressed fully equipped airfields were used. The nature of the Dakota freight
carried outbound — ammunition, petrol, general
war supplies etc — prevented the aircraft carrying the Red Cross insignia. Quite often we had to
night stop, or carry supplies from one base to
another, often visiting several before we
eventually picked up our load of casualties. One
day I landed in five different countries —
Belgium, France, Holland, Germany, and
Denmark — before heading back home.

'On one flight the Dakota was in trouble with an engine on fire — luckily we had no patients on board — and we made an emergency landing at an RAF base in Germany and crashlanded. The freight on board was cans of fuel, these all breaking loose on impact, as the Dakota overshot the runway. I managed a lift in another Dakota, bound for the UK but this landed in a bomb crater — the third attempt to get back home was lucky. With the end of the war in Europe in sight, PoW's replaced casualties, and by coincidence one of the many ferried back recognised me. It turned out he lived a short distance from my home in Wellingborough.'

Mrs Bonnie Budd, one of the many nursing orderlies involved in Casualty Air Evacuation, flew operational sorties with 233, 271 and 437 (RCAF) Squadrons from UK bases located at Down Ampney, Odiham, Western Zoyland, Benson, Thorney Island, Hurn and Eastchurch. Casualties with burns went to a hospital at Odstock, Salisbury in Wiltshire; head injuries to St Dunstan's at Radcliffe, Oxford, and spinal and skin grafting to Stoke Manderville, near Aylesbury. Canadian casualties were flown into Farnborough as the Canadian HQ was located at nearby Aldershot with its own hospital. Bonny Budd's longest flight was to Nancy in France to collect a group of SAS (Special Air Service) troops led by Col Frank who had a leg injury. They were returning from an operation behind the German lines.

Mrs Elsie Vann (née Beer) was based at RAF Down Ampney and flew with 48, 271 and 437 (RCAF) Squadrons. Her first operational sortie was on 18 June 1944, in Dakota KG592 from 48 Squadron, piloted by Sqn Ldr W. Smith, landing first at RAF Tangmere, Sussex, to pick up freight and then to B4 (Beny Sur Mer) airstrip in Normandy which was still under enemy fire, shrapnel

going through the Dakota windows. The mission was completed successfully with 18 wounded brought home safely. 'It was a wonderful feeling to bring patients and sometimes repatriated prisoners back home,' writes Elsie Vann. Most of the nursing orderlies kept a flying log-book record of their flights and 421970 Cpl Elsie Beer in her RAF Form 414 recorded 369hr 19min in Dakota transports between 7 May 1944, and 27 April 1945. On 3 May 1945, Dakota KG629 piloted by Flt Lt Stone, with Elsie Beer as nursing orderly, flew 26 Canadian casualties from RAF Down Ampney to Farnborough consisting of 16 stretcher and 10 walking cases. Canadian casualties were also landed at RAF Hartford Bridge, or Blackbushe as it was later known. The nursing orderly was responsible for loading the aircraft with casualties, and during the flight home administered oxygen or morphine as required, plus hot drinks etc. Sometimes the flight was bumpy and uncomfortable, and on occasions the Dakota had to divert due to base weather being below landing limits.

There were casualties. On 21 February 1945, Dakota FZ624 piloted by Flt Lt Soutley was lost, the crew including a nursing orderly M. Walsh. Margaret Campbell, a Scot, was posted missing presumed killed whilst on nursing orderly duties.

The Assault on Europe

During early 1944, as the time drew near for the detailed planning for the invasion of Europe, one of the major considerations was to ensure an adequate supply of aircraft for the airborne operations and preliminary training. Within RAF Transport Command, 38 Group was obviously not going to be large enough, with only 180 aircraft, to cope with the demands likely to be made upon it and so the formation of a new Group (No 46) was authorised. This group was formed on 17 January 1944, within Transport Command, with a unit equipment of 150 Dakota transports, with HQ at Harrow Wealdstone, Middlesex. Very little space was available, so in February HQ was moved to the 'Cedars' Uxbridge Road. Air Commodore Fiddament was appointed Air Officer Commanding.

In view of the very limited time remaining and the fact that scarcely any of the crews were experienced in airborne operations basic training was started immediately by the two original squadrons of the group — 271 Squadron at Doncaster and 512 Squadron at Hendon. Owing to the unsuitable location and weather of the airfields at Doncaster and Hendon, 271 and 512 were transferred to new stations allocated to the group. Three new airfields — Broadwell, Down Ampney and Blakehill Farm, had been intended for use by USAAF medium bombers and whilst the runways, perimeter tracks and dispersal areas were good, the remainder was far from complete. The airfield nearest completion was Broadwell and 512 Squadron moved in, and early in February 1944 No 575 Squadron was formed by taking a flight from 512 Squadron. No 271 Squadron moved south to Down Ampney on 29 February with 30 new Dakota transports, and on 1 March 46 Group was completed with the transfer of 48 Squadron to Down Ampney and 233 Squadron to Blakehill Farm. These last two were ex-Coastal Command, having taken part in the Battle of the Atlantic. With these five squadrons the group began training.

Nos 38 and 46 Groups of RAF Transport Command, who were to carry the 6th Airborne Division to Normandy on D-Day, had undergone

Below: Dakota Mk III FZ566 (ex-C-47A-1-DK 42-92314 c/n 12101) drops British paratroops on the practice dropping zone located at Tatton Park, near the base of No 1 Parachute Training School at RAF Ringway, Manchester. *MoD*

many weeks of intensive training which culminated in Exercise 'Mush', carried out on 21 April over an area stretching from the Severn estuary to the borders of Wiltshire and Oxfordshire. Such exercises, of which the frequency increased as the great day drew near, were difficult and dangerous; both Lt-Gen Browning, commanding the airborne forces, and Air Vice-Marshal Hollinghurst, commanding the air transport groups, took the view that it was better to run considerable risks rather than to send half-trained and inexperienced soldiers and aircrews into battle. This decision was abundantly justified, for the task facing the groups was heavy; not only must the 6th Airborne Division be taken to the right place, it had also to arrive at precisely the right moment, if surprise, essential to success, was to be achieved. Correct timing was essential. The use of different types of aircraft and different types of combinations complicated matters because of the different speeds.

On D-Day, 6 June 1944, a total of 108 Dakotas from Nos 48, 233, 271, 512 and 575 Squadrons, under the operational control of 46 Group, dropped the main body of the 3rd Parachute Brigade in Normandy, and also towed Airspeed Horsa gliders into action. Seventy-one of these Dakotas conveyed the principal group to drop zone 'V' by the River Dives, but only 17 aircraft dropped their troops on the correct spot, nine within one mile and 11 within one and a half miles. The landing of the Horsa gliders, one of them within fifty yards of the swing bridge across the Caen canal was successful. The 5th Parachute Brigade, taken into action by 129 aircraft from both 38 and 46 Groups, found their dropping zone correctly marked; 123 aircraft dropped their loads accurately, though a high wind scattered the paratroops far and wide. Out of the 2,125 paratroops belonging to this brigade, 2,026 were dropped and 702 out of 755 containers. A total of 264 aircraft and 98 glider combinations were despatched by the two groups. Altogether, 4,310 paratroops were dropped and gliders carried 493 troops, 17 guns, 44 jeeps and 55 motorcycles. Seven aircraft and 22 gliders were lost.

D-Day closed with Operation 'Mallard', the flying of 256 gliders bearing reinforcements and stores to the British 6th Airborne Division. A total of 246 of them arrived at the correct landing zone. Close fighter escort was provided to this slow-moving force towed to its destination by the tugs from 38 and 46 Groups — the gliders landed just north of Ranville and between Ouistreham and Benouville. The operation was successful, 95% of the gliders reaching their destination, much to the joy of the hard-pressed men of the 6th Airborne Division.

Sergeant Bryan Tomblin, Glider Pilot, 'E' Squadron, Glider Pilot Regiment recalls his impression of flying to Arnhem:
'On 6 June 1944, I was privileged to be the co-pilot of a Horsa glider which formed part of the largest invasion force ever known — when 17,000 airborne troops took part in the D-Day landings. Towed by Dakotas from RAF Down Ampney we spearheaded the glider force to land near the Orne Canal on the left flank of the invasion beaches. The main landing took place at 21.05hrs on 5 June, and despite mines and anti-glider poles the airborne troops fulfilled their task and ensured that no attack was mounted against the invading armies. The following morning the glider pilots were withdrawn, having been relieved by Lord Lovat's Commandos. We returned to the UK, in assault landing craft, to prepare to mount another glider operation then being planned, this time near Caen, but it never came to anything.

'Between D-Day and Arnhem a considerable number of airborne operations were planned, including a landing near Paris to cut off the retreating German armies, but Gen Patton and his US 3rd Army rendered it unnecessary by their swift advance on the Allies southern flank.

'Much has been written about the landing at Arnhem, or Operation Market Garden, but briefly the British and American Airborne Forces set to capture three important bridges. The 101st US Airborne Division was to capture the Eindhoven-Grave road and the bridge at Grave, the 82nd US Airborne Division was to secure the road from Grave to Nijmegen and capture the bridge at Nijmegen, and the British 1st Airborne Division was given the task of securing the bridge over the Rhine at Arnhem. History books contain the details of this massive operation, critics have gloried in finding various reasons for its

Below: The view from the cockpit of a Airspeed Horsa glider showing clearly the tow-line and the Dakota tug. The circumference of the rope was 4in and it was 350ft long. The Army glider pilot required considerably training before he was passed out as fully qualified. He flew fully equipped to go into battle once he had landed his steed. *Fox Photos*

Above: Two senior officers watch as a mass formation of no less than 36 Dakotas from 46 Group RAF Transport Command practice for the real thing — D-Day 6 June 1944. *IWM*

shortcomings, and the film *A Bridge Too Far* showed with spectacular camera work various aspects of the Battle of Arnhem.

'My humble account of this battle and after begins once again on the runway at RAF Down Ampney, where once again we had gone through the usual briefing, loadings and confinement to camp restrictions. At 09.40 hours on Sunday, 17 September 1944, our CO Maj Peter Jackson rolled down the runway behind the Dakota, and we were already moving after him as he lifted off. On this day each "train" got airborne every 35 seconds. We gathered speed slowly, because the Airspeed Horsa was loaded with 24 soldiers of the Air Landing Brigade (Kings Own Scottish Borderers), two motorcycles and medical stores. We became airborne and kept the glider down to allow the Dakota to ease off the ground, and begin to climb. At that moment one of the tug's engines lost power and it became debatable whether we would have to go round rather than over Cricklade Church spire. We managed to skim over the top and commence our slow climb in rather bad visibility. The tug crew assured us over the inter-com that the dicky engine seemed OK and we settled down for our three hour flight to Arnhem.

'The cloud was bothersome, so, after warning the tug captain, we adopted the low-tow position, where we fly under the slipstream of the aircraft and bring into play an "angle of dangle" instrument. Flying in cloud on low-tow was not easy, with the glider bucking and tossing in the bumpy air associated with cloud flying.

'Eventually we emerged from the cloudy conditions, and were now flying over Hertfordshire, then Suffolk. We left the English coast with Aldeburgh on our port side and the North Sea stretched in front of us. Our passengers seemed cheerful enough, although I suspected some had been sick or were about to be sick. The North Sea looked grey, rough, cold and uninviting, although Air Sea Rescue launches had mounted a massive operation to haul us out of the water, if necessary.

'Our Horsa was not an easy aircraft to fly — and the work necessitated each of us to take very regular turns at flying the old bus — and don't forget we were dressed in full Army uniform ready to assume our role as fighting soldiers upon landing. It was a biggish aircraft with an 88ft wing span, 67ft long fuselage with an all-up weight of 15,500lb of which nearly 7,000lb was payload.

'By now we were flying over the flooded parts of Holland, and it was comforting to see scores of Typhoons and Spitfires acting as escorts. These soon dealt with AA fire which floated prettily up towards us, bursting into black puffs of harmless looking smoke. Visibility was pretty good now, and after more flying we approached the Rhine from the South West with most of Arnhem on the north bank. We checked the aerial photographs for the river, the town, the wooded areas and I pointed out the Arnhem Bridge to Alec. We spotted our zone by the corner of a wood and then pulled off from tow. There was the usual jerk, the diminishing wind noise and the sight of the tug doing a shallow dive with the rope stream-

ing behind it. We pulled the nose of the Horsa up to lose flying speed to attain our best gliding speed of about 85mph. A turn to port and our zone was coming up fast. Alec applied half-flap, and we kept it there until we cleared a row of tall poplars. Full flap on, and nose down. The rear of the glider seemed to kick upwards with the effect of those huge flaps, and we were diving steeply towards the ground. We flattened out just above the ground, after skimming the trees, and with the usual clatter and banging we raced along the ground heading straight for another glider and the corner of the wood. Evasive action on the brakes saw us safely stopped. No land mines or mortar fire, but dry mouths.

The KOSBs were out like shots from a gun, and shouted thanks to us. They manhandled the motor bicycles and stores out of the main door, and as we were not carrying jeeps or guns on this trip we didn't have to remove the rear fuselage to get them out. A strange sound of wailing floated across the field — was it a German secret weapon — no, it was a bagpiper of the KOSB standing at the rendezvous and making it easy for his troops to muster in that area. It was now a hot autumn day, the sun was shining and it was relatively quiet and unwarlike — one felt one had intruded on a quiet Dutch Sunday without an invitation.'

One of the pilots flying a Dakota in the airborne armada to Arnhem was Wg Cdr W. E. Coles, who, on 6 June 1944, had relinquished command of 117 Squadron in SEAC. Earlier that year, during Operation 'Thursday' he had flown many missions in and out of all the airstrips located behind the Japanese lines. Bill Coles arrived in the UK during July 1944 and took over command of 233 Squadron based at Blakehill Farm. On Operation 'Market Garden' he flew Dakota Mk III KG559 towing an Airspeed Horsa glider. He was one of the many who gained decorations for their gallant part in this fateful operation, and was awarded the DSO. Four days later, on a resupply mission his Dakota was damaged by flak, his wireless operator Flg Off Sharpe was wounded and he was forced to land at airstrip B56 (Brussels Evère).

The second lift to Arnhem, on 18 September, was delayed five hours by the UK weather. By then the situation in the battlefield had deteriorated. On this occasion 296 tugs and gliders took off, 200 landed in one zone and 69 in the other. One tug aircraft was lost and another Dakota, from 575 Squadron based at Broadwell, was brought back to the UK by the second navigator — WO A. E. Smith — the pilot being killed and first navigator wounded — and successfully landed, though Smith had never flown an aircraft before. Despite mounting casualties, and an almost impossible task, the supply aircraft continued day after day in their gallant if fruitless efforts. The operation cost 38 and 46 Group a total of 55 aircraft with a further 320 damaged by flak and seven by fighters, the majority of these being Dakotas. On 21 September, 48 Squadron lost six Daks — all Mk IIIs — FZ620, KG346, KG350, KG404, KG417 and KG579. Between

Above: Transports from 271 Squadron RAF parked on an airstrip in Belgium after bringing in supplies from the UK. On the return journey they carried casualties, or POWs. The squadron was part of 46 Group Transport Command and based at Down Ampney. *IWM*

17 and 30 September, a total of 20,190 troops had been dropped by parachute, 13,781 had landed in gliders, and 905 were landed on a strip made ready by the preceding airborne troops. In addition to this total 5,230 tons of equipment and supplies, 1,927 vehicles, and 568 artillery pieces, were transported by air. In all, the supporting air forces flew over 7,800 sorties with supplies.

As operations in Europe had now moved further eastwards, the range for aircraft based in the UK was greatly increased and it was decided to move some of the transport squadrons to East Anglia to facilitate operations. This move took place during October 1944. The 46 Group squadrons were moved to airfields in Essex. Gosfield became the base for 271, 512 and 575 Squadrons, and Birch the new base for 48, 233 and 437 (RCAF) Squadrons, all equipped with 20 Dakotas per squadron. From these two bases 46 Group flew the British 6th Airborne Division on Operation 'Varsity' on 24 March 1945.

Operation 'Varsity' was the most successful airborne operation carried out to date, and its brilliant results reflected the great strides made in this aspect of warfare since the Normandy landings, nine months earlier. The 6th Airborne Division had been carried in 669 transports and 429 gliders from 38 and 46 Groups, with the support already mentioned from US 9th Troop Carrier Command. By this time the 2nd Tactical Air Force was being supplied with petrol, oil and ammunition, by the 280 transport aircraft available. During April 1945, 46 Group with its Dakotas carried nearly 7,000 tons of supplies. Nor did the transports return empty, for they brought back to the UK 27,277 Allied PoW's and 5,986 casualties, during this period.

In May 1945 the struggle for Europe was over, but the Dakotas of RAF Transport Command were required elsewhere. The SEAC Commander, Lord Louis Mountbatten, required more Dakota squadrons to assist with the final Allied onslaught against the Japanese in the Far East. Bomber squadrons were re-equipped with Dakotas, and veteran units such as 48 and 233 Squadrons ceased duties with 46 Group, and commenced training for transport duties in the warmer climate of SEAC.

They bade farewell to the 'Red Devils', a name bestowed on the British airborne troops by the enemy in March 1943. These were the valiant men who wore maroon berets and the badge of 'Pegasus', the winged horse and its rider, brandishing a lance, singularly appropriate. It is the emblem of which they remain justly proud to this day.

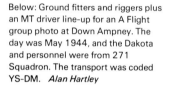

Below: Ground fitters and riggers plus an MT driver line-up for an A Flight group photo at Down Ampney. The day was May 1944, and the Dakota and personnel were from 271 Squadron. The transport was coded YS-DM. *Alan Hartley*

In RAAF Service

A Douglas Dakota from 36 Squadron RAAF is parked after landing on a dirt strip somewhere in the Pacific theatre of operations during World War 2.
RAAF

On the eve of the Japanese seven-point assault against Hawaii, Wake Island, Guam, the Philippines, Hong Kong, Thailand and Malaya, the RAAF had on strength some 536 aircraft. This included a number of transports: 24 Lockheed Hudsons in Malaya and Singapore, 53 Hudsons with front-line units in Australia and 126 Ansons in Australia with reserve units. In spite of combat losses and other attritions, the RAAF slowly increased its strength by absorbing aircraft, including transports, belonging to Allied units retreating from South East Asia, and by impressing Australian civil airliners like the Douglas DC-3 into service. However, the main source of aircraft operated by the RAAF during World War 2 was the USA which supplied over 100 Douglas C-47s. It is not generally known that as a result of the steady flow of aircraft, both from the USA and the United Kingdom, Australia ended the war with the fourth largest Allied Air Force, after the USA, the USSR and the United Kingdom.

The RAAF Douglas C-47 Dakotas carried identification numbers assigned in compliance with provisions of the Australian Air Board's Agenda No 121 dated 12 August 1921. These ident numbers were suffixed by the letter 'A' and comprised two sets of digits. The first set identified the aircraft type, whilst the second identified the individual aircraft within a type. For example A65-1 indicates the first aircraft of the 65th type listed — Douglas Dakota — being A65-1 Douglas C-47-DL ex-USAAF 41-38713 c/n 6172. It is of interest to note that this aircraft which was delivered to the RAAF in 1943, disappeared carrying medical evacuees whilst on a flight from Biak to Australia. It was discovered at 13,500 ft on a jagged mountain range in West Irian some 25 years later.

RAAF Dakotas commenced operations during February 1943, and included three C-47-DLs (A65-1/3/4) followed by 50 C-47A-DL and C-47A-DKs (A65-2 and A65-5 to A65-59) and 65 C-47B-DKs (A65-60 to A65-124). In addition 24 Douglas C-47s, C-49s, C-50s and C-53s were operated on loan from the USAAF, these not being allocated RAAF serial numbers. Four ex-Australian National Airways (ANA) Douglas DC-3s were impressed by the RAAF between September 1939 and mid-1940 and allocated the RAAF serials A30-1/2/3/4. A total of 10 ex-Eastern Air Lines Douglas DC-2s were impressed by the RAAF during 1940/41 and allocated the RAAF serials A30-5 through A30-14. World War 2 Dakota units included Nos 33, 34, 35, 36, 37 and 38 Squadrons, plus No 1 Comm Unit.

During the first two years of World War 2 the demand for air transport in the RAAF was small, and all requirements were handled mainly by sea and rail. By December 1941 when the Japanese entered the war, the RAAF was still devoid of transport squadrons, but after the early successes of the Japanese and their rapid and alarming approach towards the mainland of Australia, the need for air transport became far more urgent. The three Australian services increased in size, and the arrival of large numbers of US forces into Australia threw an even greater strain on the resources then available, whilst the need to move personnel and materials to the battle areas in the shortest possible time became an urgent necessity.

Shortages of suitable aircraft had prevented any rapid expansion of air transport in the RAAF, but during February and March 1942, four transport squadrons were formed. The first was No 34 located at Darwin on 6 February

Below: Delivered to Eastern Airlines in October 1934 as NC13737, this DC-2-112 c/n 1287 went to the RAAF on 8 November 1940 as A30-5, radio c/s VH-RCH. It served with 36 Squadron coded RE-H and finally crashed at Seven Mile Strip, Port Moresby, New Guinea on 15 September 1942.
Australian War Memorial

1942; No 33 formed on 16 February 1942, at Townsville. Two more were formed on 11 March 1942: No 35 at Pearce, and No 36 at Laverton. It is this latter squadron which is now described as a fine example of how the RAAF utilised to the full their Douglas military transport aircraft, during and after World War 2.

Flt Lt W. H. Heath RAAF, was appointed temporary commanding officer of 36 Squadron on 17 March 1942, and five days later the unit commenced to function with a personnel strength of two officers, 24 other ranks, and a single Douglas DC-2 transport — A30-14 c/n 1288 delivered to Eastern Air Lines during October 1934 as a DC-2-112 NC13738 and imported to Australia on 1 May 1941 with R/T call-sign VH-CRH. During the following months personnel strength was increased to three officers and 45 other ranks, with aircraft multiplied to three with the addition of DC-2s A-30-11 (c/n 1286 ex-Eastern NC13736 imported to Australia on 30 March 1941 and allocated R/T call-sign VH-CRE) and A30-13 (c/n 1373 ex-Eastern NC14970, R/T call-sign VH-CRG). DC-2 A30-12 arrived with 36 Squadron from Parkes on 28 April and was found to be incompletely modified for use as an emergency air ambulance. Modification was completed by the units riggers. A further DC-2 (A30-10 c/n 1372 ex-Eastern NC14969 imported 17 March 1941, R/T call-sign VH-CRD) was delivered on 26 May and 36 Squadron became the first and only RAAF squadron to be equipped with efficient transport aircraft. During this initial period the aircrews were kept busy and any serviceable aircraft was loaded and despatched immediately. Ground crews maintained the aircraft under the most difficult conditions, all members working round the clock whilst one was in the hangar. Lack of

equipment and spare parts caused an added burden to the difficulties.

Prior to June 1942, the major part of the squadron's operations consisted of flights from Laverton to Batchelor, Northern Tasmania, with stores and equipment from No 1 Aircraft Depot. However, during June the squadron flew occasional trips to Maylands, Western Australia, and on one occasion transported armour plate to 100 Squadron encamped at Mareeba, Queensland. On 14 July 1942, 36 Squadron came under the operational control of the newly formed Air Transport Command, Directorate of Air Transport, Allied Air Forces. As a result of this change, all freight was picked up at fixed control points. The control point for the southern area was Essendon, so all freight from Victoria to be transported by air was given a priority by ATC and delivered to the Air Transport Control Officer located at Essendon, where it was loaded on Douglas aircraft in its order of priority. Such freight was flown to its final destination by either the RAAF or USAAF, according to aircraft availability.

Due to the fact that 36 Squadron aircraft had to fly to Essendon to pick up freight, and that Australian National Airways did all the 240 hour and complete overhauls on the DC-2s, a decision was made to move the squadron to Essendon for convenience. This move commenced on 16 July and was completed the following day, the unit taking over the offices, stores and hangar space recently vacated by No 1 Communication Flight which had moved out to Laverton. Messing facilities were shared with USAAF personnel from the 22nd Troop Carrier Squadron. During August the squadron became responsible as a master depot for Douglas transport spares, and as these arrived it was obvious more storage

Below: Senior officers and staff from HQ 1st Army await orders prior to departure from Mareeba, Queensland, on 28 September 1944 for a flight to Port Moresby by RAAF Dakotas. The Dakota depicted is A65-4, radio c/s VH-CTD, coded RE-G from 36 Squadron and delivered to the RAAF on 26 March 1943.
Australian War Memorial

Above: An RAAF Dakota from 113 Squadron, coded LO-T, is seen flying over the dense Burmese jungle on its way to the Arakan to drop supplies to Fourteenth Army. Australian personnel were prominent in the many Dakota squadrons operated by SEAC. *RAAF*

space was needed. The USAAF were approached, and loaned a section of one of their hangars.

On 11 August 1942, a sixth Douglas DC-2 was allocated to the squadron, this being A30-9 (c/n 1292 ex-Eastern NC13782 imported 3 February 1941, with R/T call-sign VH-CRK). Also by this time two de Havilland DH84s (A34-3 and A34-11) one DH86 (A31-1) and a single Beechcraft C-17B (ex-VH-UXP) had been received by the unit. This increase in aircraft necessitated an application for an increase in personnel. The utmost serviceability was demanded by ATC HQ at this time, as every available aircraft was being used to fly men and material into Port Moresby. Maintenance crews were working round the clock to ensure that no aircraft was held up longer than necessary. The CO became quite concerned over the health of his flying personnel. With only six pilots including the CO the squadron was averaging 130 flying hours per month. Towards the end of the month the situation improved slightly when a conversion and a posting in gained two more pilots.

During August 1942 ATC moved to Brisbane, followed by the 22nd Troop Carrier Squadron the following month, leaving 36 Squadron the sole occupant on the base. However, at the end of the month the RAAF moved in 256 personnel from No 11 Elementary Flying Training School for an indefinite period to continue their training which had been interrupted by heavy rains at their training base at Benalla. Another Douglas DC-2 was issued to the squadron on 14 September, this being A30-5 (c/n 1287 ex-Eastern NC13737 imported on 8 November 1940). The aircraft was collected from Archerfield, Queensland, and the crew received orders to proceed as directed by ATC in Brisbane. It was loaded and departed for Port Moresby the same day, but crashed and burnt out whilst landing at Seven Mile Strip. The entire crew was killed and the aircraft and cargo were a total loss. This was the squadron's first

major fatality. On 8 November Flt Lt W. G. Heath RAAF relinquished command of the squadron, and the following day Sqn Ldr G. H. Purvis RAAF arrived from No 1 OTU and assumed command.

During this period the squadron was engrossed with the multitudinous chores of a unit preparing for a move, which was more or less completed on 27 November when the rear echelon was deleted and the advance party departed from Essendon for a new operational base at Stock Route Strip, Townsville. The squadron, less the rear echelon, completed its move on 11 December and immediately commenced freighting personnel, vital mail and general supplies to Port Moresby and Maple, as well as continued flights with freight on the mainland. On 3 January 1943, 42 airmen from 36 Squadron rear echelon were posted to Parafield, South Australia, where they became members of the reformed 34 Squadron. Meanwhile a detached flight of 36 Squadron remained at Essendon, and the units strength was considerably enhanced on 19 January 1943, when five Douglas C-53s were assigned, on loan from the USAAF. These were VH-CCB c/n 4823 ex-41-20053; VH-CCC c/n 4824 ex-41-20054; VH-CDJ c/n 4120 ex-41-7698 (actually a C-50); VH-CDK c/n 4119 ex-41-7697 (another C-50); and VH-CWA c/n 4840 ex-41-20070. The two C-50s commenced life on the Douglas production line as DC-3-277D airliners for American Airlines but were procured by the USAAF before delivery. VH-CDJ was named *Waltzing Matilda* and VH-CWA *Wonga Hill*. These were the first Dakota types to be operated by the RAAF and proved a valuable asset. Much valuable experience was gained on these new aircraft, and on receipt a training programme was initiated to convert DC-2 captains. This proved very successful and as more of the new Douglas C-47s became available to the RAAF captains from the squadron were posted to take delivery of new aircraft and proceed to squadrons which were being re-equipped with the type. It is of historical interest to note that all five of the USAAF Douglas C-47s loaned to 36 Squadron survived World War 2.

A detachment from 36 Squadron commenced operations in New Guinea on 1 June 1943, transporting personnel, vital mail and general freight to the various headquarters and camps occupied by allied forces. On 10 June suggestions were put to the Air Board with reference to the training of DC-2 pilots for the Parachute Training Unit. It was suggested that DC-2s from 36 Squadron should be allocated to the PTU so that its training programme could be finalised. Sqn Ldr H. Purvis, accompanied by Flt Lt F. Cook, arrived at the unit on 21 June and discussed a standardised method of converting pilots to the DC-2. Cook remained with the PTU in order to implement the conversion, and to receive instruction in the art of dropping paratroops from the DC-2. During the following month B Flight was attached to

Richmond to provide DC-2 aircraft for use by the PTU as required, and for training and transport duties. On 21 June the squadron once more changed its operational base, moving to Garbutt or 23 Operational Base Unit as it was then known. On 15 December 23 OBU became known as RAAF Station Garbutt, Townsville.

During 1944 the squadron underwent many changes. B Flight ceased to function as a detached flight at Richmond on 8 May. A Flight terminated its functions at Essendon on 6 August, and the detachment operating in New Guinea ceased on 30 September. Flying for the month of August 1944, showed a record number of 2,989hr 15min. A comparison of figures show the squadron's efforts had really increased since November 1942.

November and December, 1942 — 117,160 miles flown, 134,958lb carried.

January to December, 1943 — 2,369,590 miles flown, 18,573,361lb carried.

January to August, 1944 — 2,691,635 miles flown, 25,374,720lb carried.

During this period some 100,535 personnel were carried.

On 3 October 1944, the Directorate of Air Transport was disbanded and operational control of RAAF air transport was delegated to RAAF HQ by the Commander, AAF South West Pacific Area. All USAAF squadrons and civil airlines previously under DAT were taken over by the US 5298th Troop Carrier Wing. No 36 Squadron had operated under the DAT organisation since March 1942. The cooperation received and equipment made available to the squadron were always of the highest order. During the month all aircraft operated on loan from the USAAF were returned and 12 new RAAF Dakotas were on strength. Some 75% of the operational flying was carried out from Townsville to New Guinea and across the New Guinea mountains.

The squadron assisted with other unit moves during October. During a base move from Higgins to Tadji for 37 Squadron which commenced on 20 October for six days, five Daks from 36 Squadron and three from 34 Squadron plus another three from 35 Squadron were employed in the operation. A movement of No 82 Squadron from Townsville was commenced on 27 October. Four squadron Dakotas assisted by aircraft from 34 and 35 Squadrons again participated. During January 1945, the squadron had two Dakotas continually based at Tadji where they carried out supply dropping tasks to Army personnel in the area. On 26 January Dakota A65-50 VH-CIF proceeded to Bougainville for supply dropping. Army officers based at Tadji informed the squadron that the percentage of air drop recovery was as high as 98% and considered the operations highly successful. From the aircrew point of view, the supply dropping missions created an added interest, and gave them a break from scheduled runs.

The squadron's scheduled run to Noemfoor, was extended to Morotai during January, this extending the round trip to four days for completion. During February 1945, Dakota VH-CUF A65-34 failed to return from a supply dropping mission in the Aitape area. The pilot, Sqn Ldr Jackson was seriously injured, the co-pilot Flt Lt Matthews, died of wounds in Tadji hospital, and the navigator Flt Sgt Campbell was killed outright. Of the three supply droppers on board and two passengers, only one supply dropper survived. The aircraft crashed in enemy territory and was a complete loss. It was located by a patrol of commandos whose personnel performed an outstanding feat in the rescue of the survivors.

In spite of the number of adverse incidents which considerably interfered with the serviceability of squadron aircraft, the high percentage of 75.4% was held for April 1945.

The squadron's flying effort received a serious setback on 10 May by the crash of VH-CIG

Above: Flying at treetop height this Dakota — A65-48 radio c/s VH-CID coded RE-W from 36 Squadron — was an ex-C-47A-20-DK 42-93198 c/n 13083 and is seen operating in the Wewak-Aitape area during 1945. *Australian War Memorial*

A65-39, whilst it was carrying out supply dropping operations in the Aitape area in New Guinea. The crew, consisting of Flt Lt Akers, F/Sgt Lawson and Sgt McInroy, together with the crew of supply droppers, were all killed. The Dakota crashed into the side of a mountain near Housecapp and was a complete loss. It was later located by a native patrol.

Squadron serviceability throughout June rose to 83.9% which was attributed to an increase of fitters and other ground staff. This was despite a shortage of tools for the fitters which hampered their efforts towards maximum serviceability. During the month three Dakotas were on a special detachment to Morotai, where they flew a series of shuttle flights out of the area. A feeling of great satisfaction was felt throughout the squadron during July 1945, for a job well done, when it received congratulations from the CO 3rd Australian Army Division for the excellent work carried out whilst supply dropping in the Bougainville area. Time was fast running out for the Japanese aggressors, their advance had been held and turned back. The Allies were triumphant on all fronts, and it was a far cry back to the hectic and soul destroying days when they had struggled to organise their last resources and build up their strength for the long fight back. Coming into being during those early days of the South West Pacific war, the RAAF transport squadrons had more than proved their worth, and the success of the New Guinea campaign was in a large measure dependent on the untiring efforts of the squadrons of Douglas transports. In particular 36 Squadron had built up a flying record, second to none, and the major part of it was carried out in the New Guinea area, or from the mainland to New Guinea, carrying essential war materials and personnel to the forward areas, bringing out wounded and other personnel, and carrying out supply dropping operations.

On 1 August 1945, the squadron moved to Garbutt, and with the cessation of hostilities during the month it was kept very busy. It operated over the extended lines of com-

munications and crews were all keen to participate in the landing of occupation troops on enemy territory. They experienced the utmost satisfaction in being privileged to be one of the transport units involved in bringing home released PoWs, thus ending for these heroes a long period of privation and imprisonment. Two Dakota aircraft were based at Tadji, two at Morotai, one at Bougainville, and two were engaged in carrying the first section of paratroops to occupy Singapore, with a further two standing by in case they were required. The Bougainville detached flight ceased on 24 September, and the Tadji detachment also ceased during the month. However, Dakotas from Morotai were moved to Singapore and were operating out of Kalang airfield whilst one Dak per week was engaged on a mail run to Lae. The humane work concerned with the evacuation of POWs and internees from Singapore received recognition during October 1945, when 36 Squadron was praised by Lord Louis Mountbatten and Air Chief Marshal Sir Keith Park, for the part it played in the operation. The RAAF transport squadrons, including No 36, had moved 6,500 PoWs and over 1,000,000lb of freight from Singapore to the evacuation centres. By the end of the month all squadron detachments outside the mainland ceased to function.

On 1 November 1945, Dakotas A65-117 (VH-RGE), A65-118 (VH-RGF), A65-119 (VH-RBB) and A65-120 (VH-RGH) were allocated to 36 Squadron Air Ambulance Flight from No 2 Air Ambulance Unit at Archerfield which was disbanded. Aircrew and ground personnel posted in with the new transports brought the squadron strength up to 379 personnel and 20 aircraft. During January 1946, detachments were established at Darwin, Ambon and Morotai with the latter providing a tri-weekly courier service to Tokyo and Hiroshima. Two Dakotas assisted in the movement of 93 Squadron from Marromine to Iwakuni, Japan, and in turn the Beaufighters of 93 Squadron were acting as navigation aircraft for a flight of single-engined fighters being transferred to Japan.

For many years to come both 36 Squadron and the Dakota soldiered on giving yeoman service to the RAAF. Twenty members of 36 Squadron departed Kingsford Smith Airport, Mascot, on 25 August 1948, destined for HQ London to participate in Operation 'Pelican' which provided Commonwealth crews who gave assistance to the Allied effort for the supply of food and essentials to the stricken populace of Berlin. The RAAF supplied 30 Dakota crews to this effort. RAAF Dakotas serviced in Malaya with Operation 'Firedog'; in Korea supporting 77 Squadron, maintained a detachment in Japan, and up to 1981 still had 14 aircraft on the RAAF inventory. There is no doubt at all that the old 'Gooney Bird' will remain long in the thoughts of all those in the RAAF who flew and operated this great workhorse of the air.

Below: When Australian Prime Minister Chifley visited his troops at Lae on 23 December 1945, he used this RAAF Dakota from the Governer-General's Flight operated by 34 Squadron. It is A65-123 radio c/s VH-RGK which later went to the Royal Australian Navy as N2-123. *Australian War Memorial*

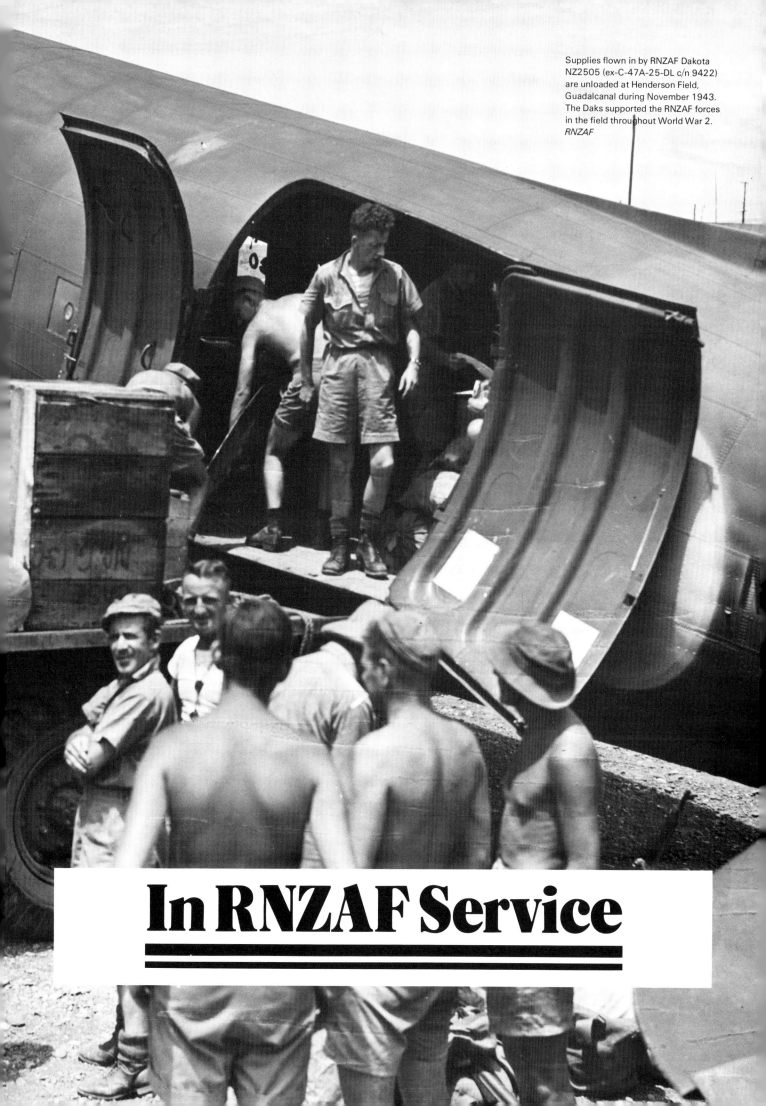

Supplies flown in by RNZAF Dakota NZ2505 (ex-C-47A-25-DL c/n 9422) are unloaded at Henderson Field, Guadalcanal during November 1943. The Daks supported the RNZAF forces in the field throughout World War 2. *RNZAF*

In RNZAF Service

With the promise of transport aircraft to be supplied during 1943, preparations were made at Whenuapai to form the first RNZAF Dakota squadron. Sqn Ldr Lucas DFC, who had returned to New Zealand after completing two operational tours in Europe, was appointed to command the new unit. The first Douglas C-47-DL (NZ3501, ex-USAAF 42-32885 c/n 9111) was flown out from the USA by an American delivery crew, arriving at Whenuapai towards the end of March 1943. By the end of May the first batch of six Douglas C-47s had arrived safely, supplemented by five Lockheed C-60 Lodestars which arrived by sea during June. On 1 June 1943, No 40 Squadron RNZAF was officially formed, its mission being to carry aircrew, ground staff, mail and urgent freight, in that order of priority, between the home base in New Zealand and the forward areas in the Pacific war.

To assist in the delivery of aircraft from the USA a Pacific ferry flight had been formed earlier, in April 1943, commanded by Wg Cdr R. J. Cohen. This flew the aircraft from the US or Hawaii to New Zealand; Douglas Dakotas for the transport squadron and Consolidated PBY Catalinas for the maritime squadrons, were flown direct from the west coast of the US by New Zealand crews. Lockheed PV-1 Harpoons for the bomber-reconnaissance squadrons were generally shipped to Kaneohe in Hawaii, assembled there by the US Navy, and then flown to New Zealand. During June a small RNZAF detachment was stationed at Kaneohe to assist the US Navy, but in September 1943 this was withdrawn, and the Pacific ferry flight was absorbed by 40 Squadron which took over the responsibilities.

For the first two months after forming, 40 Squadron Dakotas operated only as and when required. The irregular flying hours which resulted made it impossible to plan the maintenance of the aircraft in relation to flying commitments, which meant that at times there were several serviceable aircraft lying idle, and on other occasions none was available because of inspections. This difficulty was soon overcome when the squadron received its full quota of six Dakotas and five Lodestars, fully trained crews and was able to commence operating on regular schedules. The production line located at Long Beach, California during early 1943 was truly an Allied one, for in addition to C-47s for the USAAF and R4Ds for the US Navy, Dakotas were on line for the RAF, RCAF, RAAF and RNZAF.

The first schedule to be flown by 40 Squadron commenced during August 1943, with two Dakotas and four Lodestars from Whenuapai each week. One Dakota leaving on Mondays flew the route Whenuapai, Mausori, Santo, Guadalcanal, Santa, Whenuapai, arriving back at base on Thursdays; the other Dak, which left on Friday, flew the same circuit in the opposite direction. Two Lodestars, departing on Wednesdays and Sundays, operated over the same route with an additional call at Tontouta in New Caledonia. The third Lockheed transport carried passengers and freight to Norfolk Island each Friday, returning the same day. The fourth, left base every Thursday and arrived back the following Monday, carried vital mail etc to all RNZAF bases in the South Pacific. At the end of October 1943 the schedules were ammended to include Ondonga, New Georgia, where the RNZAF fighter wing had recently been established.

The increasing strength of the RNZAF in the forward area and the lengthening of its lines of communications necessitated an increase in the air transport organisation. At the end of 1943 40 Squadron received, as additional equipment, a number of Lockheed Hudsons which became available as bomber-reconnaissance squadrons re-equipped with PV-1 Venturas; and these, converted for use as troop-carriers, were employed to supplement the Lodestars and Dakotas with which the unit was originally equipped. Aircraft allocations for 1944 included an additional 15 Douglas Dakotas which were used to strengthen

Below: Spectacular World War 2 photograph of RNZAF Dakota NZ3517 (ex-C-47A-10-DK 42-92715 c/n 12546) taking off from the Piva airstrip at Bougainville in the Pacific. This was taken during January 1945. *RNZAF*

the squadron, which by August had an establishment of 16 Dakotas, 9 Lodestars, and 12 Hudson troop-carriers. At this time a new transport squadron, No 41, was formed and it took over the operation of the Lockheed Lodestars and Hudsons.

As commitments increased and aircraft became available the number of scheduled flights from Whenuapai grew steadily throughout the year. In November 1944, 40 Squadron despatched 12 Dakotas a week on regular flights extending as far as Samoa, Fiji and Guadalcanal, and 41 Squadron sent 10 aircraft a week to Guadalcanal. Bases north of Guadalcanal were served by transports controlled by No 1 (Islands) Group. A single Dakota had been stationed there at the beginning of 1944, but soon proved unable to cope with the workload, and by October the detachment had been increased to four Daks. These were augmented by a utility flight, also controlled by the Group, which operated a number of Hudsons.

A further 28 Douglas Dakota transports were allotted to the RNZAF during the first six months of 1945, and these were used to replace the Lodestars and Hudsons of 41 Squadron at Whenuapai. One other unit which was equipped with the Dakota was No 1 (Transport) OTU — Operational Training Unit — located at Onakea in June 1945, utilising six Daks from 40 Squadron. Three Dakota airframes were used at Hobsonville for ground instruction duties, these being RNZAF transports involved in accidents. An additional 49 Dakotas were allotted for the second half of 1945, and were to be used to form two more RNZAF transport squadrons. However, the end of World War 2 made the establishment of the new units unnecessary, and the orders for aircraft not yet delivered were cancelled.

During 1945 the regular transport services were augmented by a flight of four Short Sunderland flying boats, which had been made available by the British Government and which were used between New Zealand, Noumea, Santo and Lauthala Bay. They had been flown out from the United Kingdom via West Africa, South America, the USA and Honolulu, by a party under the command of Wg Cdr D. W. Baird. They were not entirely satisfactory because of servicing difficulties, but they had the advantage of being able to carry twice the payload of a Dakota.

The following figures of men, mail and equipment carried indicate the increasingly important part played by the RNZAF transport squadrons as the war progressed. In July 1943 the first month in which 40 Squadron operated on a significant scale, RNZAF aircraft carried 157 men to the Pacific Islands and repatriated 226. In the same month they took 21,000lb of freight and 6,000lb of mail forward, and brought back 7,000lb and 10,000lb respectively. A year later the corresponding figures had risen to over 700

men, 76,000lb of freight, and 28,000lb of mail on the outward flights, and 7,000 men, 66,000lb of freight and 39,000lb of mail on the homeward trip. In 1945 the figures increased still further. Altogether, from February 1943, until the end of September 1945, 37,000 passengers left from or arrived at Whenuapai by air and nearly four million pounds of freight, and one and a half million pounds of mail was carried. These figures refer only to personnel, goods and mail which passed through Whenuapai and do not take into account the very large amount of inter-island traffic.

The prompt delivery of mail by the Dakotas of the two RNZAF transport squadrons was a major factor in maintaining morale in the Pacific Islands. Letters and newspapers reached even the most distant and remote bases in a matter of days, and kept the troops in touch with what was going on at home. Also, whenever there was space available, food was carried; fresh meat, vegetables, and butter. Although limited, these supplies provided relief from the monotony of the regular ration and also helped to keep up morale. Most welcome of all, probably, were the occasional supplies of beer taken to the war front to augment spasmodic shipments by sea.

There were a series of accidents and incidents involving the RNZAF Dakotas. NZ3501 c/n 9111, the first Douglas Dakota to be delivered, collided with PV-1 Ventura NZ4518 near Whenuapai on 21 July 1945. NZ3522 c/n 25375 crashed off Savo Island, Guadalcanal on 12 July, 1945. NZ3526 c/n 26007 was posted missing between Santo, New Hebrides and New Zealand on 25 September 1945. NZ3529 c/n 26650 crashed on take-off from Pallikulo Field, New Hebrides on 6 July 1945. NZ3536 c/n 32696 crashed at Paraparaumu on 22 May 1954. NZ3549 crashed in the sea off Hobsonville on 16 November 1950. NZ3558 c/n 34229 crashed in the Philippines on 19 December 1947. NZ3501, NZ3504 and NZ3518 became ground instructional airframes at Hobsonville.

Below: The Dakota was a jack-of-all trades with the Commonwealth air forces. The crew of this Dakota are waiting for the 'green' light to drop supplies to troops fighting in the Solomons during 1945. *RNZAF*

When World War 2 came to its abrupt conclusion in August 1945, three immediate tasks were faced by the RNZAF in the Pacific area; the repatriation of New Zealand prisoners of war from Malaya; the transport home to New Zealand of the 7,000 officers and men stationed at the various bases in the South and South-West Pacific, and the demobilisation of all personnel not required for further service.

To evacuate RNZAF personnel from Malaya, a special flight was formed within the air transport organisation at Whenuapai under the command of Sqn Ldr Pirie. Dakotas were fitted up as air ambulances; medical staffs and supplies of food, clothing and essential comforts were assembled; and a small ground staff was organised to undertake inspections at a staging post between New Zealand and Singapore. The preparations were completed within a few days of the Japanese surrender, but it was not possible for the aircraft to depart for Malaya as the relieving British forces did not enter Singapore until 5 September. The first two Dakotas eventually left New Zealand on 4 September 1945, to fly via Santo, Bougainville, Biak and Morotai to Brunei Bay in Borneo, where they were to remain until word was received that the airfield at Singapore was open. Both Dakotas, including NZ3540 c/n 32896, met with disaster at Morotai when a USAAF B-24 Liberator taxied into them, destroying NZ3540 and damaging the other. Two more replacement Dakotas were immediately flown out.

The first two RNZAF Dakotas to reach Malaya landed at Kallang airfield on 12 September. Sqn Ldr Pirie and his crew acquired a house owned by a Chinese merchant in the neighbourhood, in which they set up headquarters. Wg Cdr de Lange, the RNZAF liaison officer in India, arrived in Singapore the same day, having been delayed by a forced landing on his flight from India. Little or no information on the whereabouts of New Zealand PoWs was available, so members of the Evacuation Flight, together with war correspondents and New Zealand Film Unit cameramen, visited all PoW and internment camps on Singapore Island. As New Zealanders were found, they were brought to the flight's HQ, where they were fed, clothed, and interrogated on the possible whereabouts of other New Zealanders, and quartered until they could be put on Dakotas leaving for home.

A report came in that there were New Zealand PoWs and civilian internees in Java, Sumatra, and Thailand. As no definite information could be obtained in Singapore, a Dakota transport was sent to Batavia on 16 September to bring back any who could be found there, and some days later a Dakota flew to Bangkok and picked up 21 New Zealanders who had assembled there. At the same time others were brought in from outlying areas by Dakotas of the Royal Australian Air Force.

In the meantime, more Dakotas had arrived from Whenuapai and full scale repatriation had begun. Dakotas left Singapore for Whenuapai on 15, 16 and 17 September each carrying 16 POWs and internees, flying via Brunei Bay, Morotai, Darwin, Cloncurry and Brisbane. Up to the end of September the flight was responsible for finding and collecting all New Zealanders in the area. After that a New Zealand Army contact team arrived and took over all matters dealing with non-Air Force personnel. The RNZAF unit was then able to concentrate on its main task of flying released personnel from Singapore, where they had congregated, back home to New Zealand. By the middle of October 1945, the task was completed, and the last Dakota departed Singapore on 17 October. Altogether the Flight repatriated 156 New Zealand prisoners of war and civilian internees and two Australians.

During the Malayan anti-terrorist campaign, a detachment of 41 Squadron Dakotas was involved for over three years. It was only during 1977 that thoughts for a Dakota replacement came about, and the final retirement ceremony took place on 12 November 1977, at Ohakea when the log books of the last two Daks were ceremonially handed over to Chief of the Air Staff, Air Vice Marshal C. L. Siegert RNZAF to the lament of a lone piper, ending 34 years of Dakota service.

Right: With hostilities over came the task of repatriation flights for New Zealand PoWs. Seen at Singapore during October 1945 is RNZAF Dakota NZ3547 (ex-C-47B-35-DK 44-77146 c/n 33478) which survived the war to become a civil aircraft. *RNZAF*

Dakota Mk III FL618 coded 'DM' from 32 Operational Training Unit, seen flying over the Canadian seaboard during World War 2. This is a C-47A-1-DK 42-92258 c/n 12039 which survived the war and went to Trans Canada Airlines. *RCAF*

In RCAF Service

The Douglas C-47 Dakota first went into regular service with the Royal Canadian Air Force on 29 March 1943, when aircraft No 650 was delivered to No 12 Communications Squadron at Rockcliffe. This aircraft was constructed at the Douglas Long Beach factory with USAAF serial 42-32789 and c/n 9015. As the war progressed an ever increasing number of Dakotas were delivered, some 200 being used by the RCAF. Home based units included Nos 12 and 165 Squadron, the latter based at Sea Island, Vancouver, whilst 6 OTU at Comox was responsible for aircrew training. No 168 Squadron based at Rockcliffe delivered mail overseas in Flying Fortress and Consolidated Liberator aircraft, with Dakota detachments in England, France and North Africa for onward transportation of the vital mail.

Here in the United Kingdom, No 437 'Husky' Squadron was formed at RAF Blakehill Farm, near Cirencester, Gloucestershire, on 14 September 1944. It took part in the Arnhem operation, towing gliders and dropping supplies. In March 1945, it towed gliders during the Rhine crossing and in May moved to a base in Belgium. A detachment was based in Norway from July until November 1945, whilst the main party of the squadron was based at RAF Odiham, near Basingstoke, Hants, from August to November, by which time the squadron was reunited again. At the end of May 1946, 437 Squadron RCAF ceased operations and in mid-June flew its aircraft home to Canada, the unit being disbanded on 16 June 1946.

When Wingate's raiders set off on their epic expedition into Burma, they chose as their emblem the Chinthe, a mythical monster, half-dog, half-lion, ferocious and eternally watchful, images of which stand guard over the Burmese pagodas. When 435 Squadron RCAF began operations with its Dakotas, in support of Fourteenth Army it, too, adopted the Chinthe as the squadron badge, combining it with the motto — *Certi Provehendi*. The Chinthe squadron more than lived up to its motto. After commencing operations in December 1944, it chalked up a record unsurpassed by any other unit in the Combat Cargo Task Force in South East Asia Command (SEAC). The Chinthes followed Fourteenth Army all the way from Kawlin to Meiktila and Thazi. They flew the first Dakota to cross the Irrawaddy in support of the Fourteenth Army bridgehead. Their jump-masters played a prominent role in the airborne operation against Rangoon. They flew by day and they flew by night. They flew with and without fighter escort. They landed at airfields which were under enemy fire and at airfields whose ownership at any future moment could not be vouched for by briefing officers. They dropped on dropping zones no bigger than geranium pots. They braved Japanese fighters and ground fire to deliver their loads. But the Chinthes always delivered the goods, and they brought back cargoes of army casualties without suffering a single loss.

The squadron was one of two Royal Canadian Air Force transport units which went out to India in September 1944. Its first commanding officer was Wg Cdr T. P. Harnett. Before commencing operations, the Chinthes embarked on a programme of intensive training at Gujrat in the north of India. Particular attention was paid to paratroop exercises. In November the Chinese armies began to retreat before the hard pressing Japanese. In order to meet this situation, several of the USAAF transport squadrons supplying Fourteenth Army were hurriedly moved to the Chinese front. The Chinthe squadron was ordered to move up to fill the breach immediately. By flying 28 out of 36 hours, the squadron flew to its new base at Tulihal in Assam in little more than a day. On 19 December 1944, it was operational.

There was no surplus of air transport, and in order to keep the army supplied, it was necessary to eke the last ounce of air tonnage out of every available aircraft. On its record day the squadron flew in 199 tons of supplies, its aircraft flying as much as 13 and 14 hours per day. Turn around was cut down to an almost unbelievable fine limit. Frequently the Dakotas unloaded their 7,000lb-odd of supplies and were airborne again within 10 minutes of touching down. One enthusiastic crew established an all-time record of eight minutes for this task — that is, from touch-down to take-off. The squadron flew Christmas puddings, rum, turkeys and mail to the 14th Army on Christmas Day, which was then in the Kawlin and Yazagio area. On New Year's Day the squadron was airborne on normal supply dropping operations.

On 12 January 1945, the squadron went in force to carry out a supply drop on a DZ four miles east of the town of Shwebo, an important road junction 16 miles west of the Irrawaddy. As the Dakotas came in, they joined the dropping-circuit, until there were six or seven of them over the DZ unloading a portion of their cargo on each circuit. Sqn Ldr H. L. Coons DFC was in charge of this flight his wireless operator WO R. O.

Buckmaster, was in the astro-dome keeping a look-out for enemy aircraft. It was not long before Buckmaster warned the pilot of a Japanese Zero fighter making an attack on the Dakota. Coons cut his throttle and hit the deck — then he opened up and headed north. The Zero made four passes at the Dakota, its guns blazing each time. Cpl A. M. White, one of the groundcrew who came along as cargo 'kicker' was hit in the chest with a bullet. After the fifth attack Coons managed to break free and head for home. He arrived with the aircraft full of holes and minus four feet of wing tip. For his coolness and courage under fire, Sqn Ldr Coons was awarded a bar to his DFC.

Meanwhile the other Dakotas were hard pressed. According to reports by ground observers, there were a dozen Zeros in the circuit diving on the defenceless transports. Flg Off J. K. Ramsay in his Dakota didn't have a chance, the Zero got him first time and his aircraft plunged to earth, enveloped in flames. Only the co-pilot, Flg Off A. L. Thompson, survived. The third aircraft to be attacked was piloted by Flt Lt R. F. Simpson, the unit's only English skipper; Flg Off T. Jordan-Knox was co-pilot. The bulk of their load was ammunition — one Japanese shell properly placed and they were goners. They received a blast, LAC R. G. Evans, a groundcrew kicker, was hit in the arm. WO D. G. Cotter received a cannon shell in his abdomen and fell to the floor, groaning. Flg Off A. E. Foster, who had come along for the ride, had two bullets rip his shirt, cutting deep grooves in the flesh of his back. The ammunition caught fire, the tail caught fire, and the port engine caught fire. Foster started to get rid of the blazing ammunition, and the navigator, Flg Off L. Dumont, beat out the tail fire with his bare hands. Simpson picked out a jungle clearing and brought the blazing Dakota in for a perfect crash landing. They evacuated the blazing aircraft as fast as their legs could carry them, made Dave Cotter comfortable, while the ammunition went of in all directions. Cotter died in hospital a few days later. For his skill and courage in crash-landing under extraordinary difficult conditions, Flt Lt Simpson was awarded the DFC. The hard-pressed British troops had watched the battle above them, unable to assist their Canadian friends.

In the battle for Mandalay during March, the Chinthe squadron again figured prominently. The first Dakota to arrive dropped on a hurriedly improvised DZ at the foot of Sacred Hill. The DZ itself was approximately 50 yards wide by 100 yards long — tiny enough when you consider that at a dropping speed of 120mph an aircraft traverses 100 yards in little better than one-and-a-half-seconds. The wonders of modern bomb-sight coupled with an electro-magnetic release had no application here. The drops were made visually, and the cargo unloaded by hand, the trick being to drop as many parcels per circuit, and to drop them all accurately. The situation did not improve until Fourteenth Army captured the airfield at North Mandalay and transport aircraft were able to land supplies.

After Mandalay had been taken, the Chinthe squadron was assigned to fly out the heroic 36th Division, which had fought almost 400 miles from Myitkyina to Mandalay. At the height of the battle, the Chinthe squadron had dropped the division 50,000 cigarettes out of their own issue. They fully realised that battle is precisely the time when a man needs a cigarette most. When they flew the 36th out, the Chinthes were thanked profusely for their generosity.

The men of the Combat Cargo Task Force had to cope with other enemies than the Japanese. For a time in February 1945, vast forest fires swept through the jungles of Burma, and the Chinthes flew through the dense smoke which billowed up to 15,000ft and more, with horizontal visibility virtually nil. They had to fly over some of the worst jungle in the world and through what is unquestionably the worst weather in the world. In Burma the monsoons break near the end of May, and continue with fluctuating intensity until September. They are characterised by swiftly changing weather, heavy rainfall, and frequent and violent thunderstorms. Over the Chin Hills the storms are especially widespread and violent. Several of the Chinthe squadron Dakota pilots had unnerving experiences whilst flying during the monsoon season.

When operations ceased at Tulihal in the last days of August 1945, the Chinthes had completed just over eight months with the Combat Cargo Task Force. During those eight months the squadron had flown 29,873hr on 16,592 sorties, averaging almost 120hr per day throughout the whole period. Its Dakotas consumed over 1,760,000gal of aviation fuel and covered more than four million miles. The average Dakota flew seven hours per day. The cargo delivered totalled 27,460 tons, in addition to which 14,400 passengers and 851 casualties were carried. With meagre equipment the groundcrew worked

Below: Depicting an unusual fin flash marking this RCAF Dakota from 164 Squadron is ex-C-47-DL 42-32882 c/n 9108. It was taken on charge by the RCAF on 27 April 1943, and although struck off charge during November 1955, was retained as a ground instruction aircraft. *RCAF*

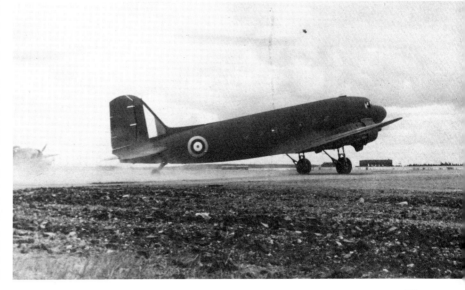

wonders. Engine changes, normally a job for repair depots were carried out in half a day and less. Serviceability during the crucial months was kept up around the 90% mark. A truly amazing figure for a tropical station reflecting the tremendous devotion of the ground crews. When they travelled as kickers as they often did, they also shared the dangers of flying. Their work on the ground was routine, tedious, exacting. But without their efforts the fine showing of the squadron would have been unattainable.

After VJ-Day, which the Chinthes celebrated at the estate of the Maharajah of Manipur, the squadron prepared to fly back from Burma to the UK. Late in August the first wave of Dakotas left Tulihal, followed at intervals by other groups, until the last departed on 11 September 1945. Their homeward course took them via Alipore, Maharajpore, Karachi, Masirah, Aden, Wadi Halfa, Lydda, El Adam, El Aouina and Istres, to RAF Down Ampney in Gloucestershire. On 31 March 1946, 435 Squadron was officially disbanded overseas, and the 25 Dakotas flown home. Canada may well be proud of its Chinthe squadron and cherish the memory of those Chinthemen who gave their lives while carrying the means of battle to the Army in Burma.

The other Royal Canadian Air Force squadron to form at Gujerat, a fighter base near the border of Kashmir, was No 436 — the first Canadian squadron to be officially created in the Far East. By November 1944, the unit was a working entity, with enough personnel and aircraft — Dakotas Mk III and Mk IV — to start intensive training for its role of air transport in direct support of units of Fourteenth Army. Like its sister squadron — No 435 — it belonged to 229 Group, part of the RAF, USAAF, RCAF, military airline known as Combat Cargo Task Force.

On 4 January 1945, the squadron was ordered to move to Kangala and be fully operational by 15 January. The 1,300-mile airlift to the new base was the longest overland move undertaken by an RCAF squadron overseas. On arrival all hands, officers included, turned to the task of unloading the Dakotas and setting up camp on the airstrip, a task hardly facilitated by the lack of drinking water and motor transport. The USAAF eased the situation by loaning the squadron a full 200gal water trailer and jeep. Considerable hill side gouging had to be done to accommodate the overflow of tentage caused by the presence of 436 personnel, plus members of the outgoing unit — 42 Squadron with Hawker Hurricanes — who had not yet vacated their premises. Kangla was situated about eight miles north-west of Imphal, Manipur, and 40 miles from the India-Burma border.

The tactical debut of 436 Squadron took place on 15 January 1945, and involved seven Dakotas transporting fuel, food and medical supplies to 33 Corps at Shwebo, 180 miles to the south-east. That day they para-dropped, free-dropped, or landed, 45 tons of payload without incident, and the fighter escort of Republic Thunderbolts around the DZ proved unnecessary. The honour of delivering the unit's first load fell to Flt Lt W. S. Robertson (captain), Sgt B. J. Vincent RAF (co-pilot) Flt Lt J. W. Dolphin, (nav) and Plt Off R. W. Eves (w/op).

It took 436 Squadron less than a week to begin making a name for itself — as the 'Elephant' squadron. On 21 and 22 January 1945, it topped all squadrons in the group in the matter of tonnage delivered, a feat it was to duplicate again and again in the next eight months. These achievements were realised in spite of two adverse factors — fog over the DZs and shortage of unloading personnel. Captains orbited the DZs for as long as two hours waiting for the valley mists to clear. Added to the unloading problem was the refusal, on religious grounds, of Shwebo's East Africans to unload meat. Whilst there was no way of controlling fog or religious convictions, something could be done about the unloading problem in general. In unit orders of 22 January there appeared the following notice: 'Groundcrew personnel are to be employed as members of aircrews to assist in off-loading cargoes. Airmen detailed will be entitled to 75cents per day crew pay whilst so employed. Duration of detail probably two weeks. It is pointed out that the work will probably be heavy and arduous. All airmen desirous of flying with aircrews are to report to the squadron Warrant Officer ... ' The appeal was well heeded. So emerged 436's version of the crewman, who also toiled in the ground environment, but was constantly on call to take to the air. When airborne, the crewman reverted from his normal trade to the duties of 'kicker', whose inflight job was to expel with vigorous footwork supply bundles through the Dakota's open door, whilst clinging for dear life to whatever hand-grip was available. For a nominal monetary increment this volunteer shared with the aircrew all the hazards of wartime operational flying over tropical jungle. Additional responsibilities included supervision of loading, inspections, refuelling, and starting up of the aircraft.

At the beginning of February 1945, two official pronouncements concerning the flying policy had been received. First, the operational tour of transport support personnel in SEAC had been extended from 500 to 700 hours. Secondly, squadrons were now restricted to 2,500 flying hours a month. The progressive spirit of the Elephant squadron was nevertheless irrepressible. In February they logged 4,182 hours; in May 4,315; in June 4,767; and in July 4,999 hours. Rebellious though this may have seemed to the hierarchy at Group HQ, it was rebellious in a healthy form, manifesting an uncommonly enthusiastic spirit. It was not the only time 436 was to overlook a regulation for the sake of increased operational output. The very next day the unit set another squadron record for tonnage delivered. In 73 sorties it airlifted 223 tons of freight alone,

representing the second hightest total for any day in the squadron's history. The mark was to stand for nearly four months. In addition to airlifting a steady flow of supplies to ground troops, evacuating casualties, and looking for their own lost aircraft, the Elephants in one two-week period moved four RAF squadrons and a Wing HQ to new locations. Occasionally they carried bombs — for some other squadron to drop. Also on behalf of other squadrons they delivered ammunition and other volatile cargo — highly inflamable aircraft fuel. During this period they cooperated with nine Curtiss C-46 Commando crews of the USAAF who were based at Tulihal, on temporary duty.

Operations continued apace, the principal points of call being Sinthe, Allagappa, Monya, Sadaung and Shwebo, most of which were newly captured airstrips within light artillery range of the front line. It was on the Allagappa airlift of 20 February that the Elephants first became enemy conscious. Returning crews warned of Japanese patrols active in the area, and all aircraft had to be off the strip by nightfall. Crews were also cautioned to watch for enemy fighters over the Allagappa district. On 26 February, crews en route to Sinthe were warned by W/T that Jap interceptors were operating in the vicinity. The Sinthe bound aircraft pressed on, however, and, as at Allagappa, no airborne opposition was met. Thus, without further untoward events, the squadron completed its first calendar month of operations. For the 28 day period they could point to some impressive statistics: 1,625 sorties, 4,182 operational hours; 4,903 tons of payload which was exclusive of 1,459 passengers and casualties.

A fatal accident befell the squadron on 14 March. Two Dakotas engaged in moving unit equipment to the new base at Akyab were standing near Mawnubyin airstrip, which serves Akyab, when a Bristol Beaufighter, making an emergency landing, hit the tail of one and crashed squarely into the other. The co-pilot of the latter aircraft, Flt Sgt E. O. England RNZAF, later died of injuries. There could well have been more casualties a week later, when airstrips in the Meiktila district came under fire from Japanese units obviously bent on recapturing them. For two crews on 21 March it was too close for comfort, Flg Off W. Davidson's aircraft absorbing three bullets near the tail and Flg Off W. J. Holland's having a fuel tank drained by one well-placed round. More shells found the Meiktila strip the following day and were probably responsible for the destruction of the control tower. At any rate, the strip had to be closed to traffic that afternoon and was not revisited by the squadron for six days.

Through most of April and May the squadron experienced an abnormal number of engine failures. Acting on orders from higher authority, 436 had switched — with misgivings — from 'T' to 'X' oil and the mounting unserviceabilities were

Far left, top to bottom:

Dakotas from 436 Squadron RCAF seen unloading at a forward airfield in Burma during 1944. The Dak on the left is KJ949 (ex-C-47B-10-DK 43-48980 c/n 26241) which survived and was stored with 12 MU in the UK during 1947 and disposed of during 1948. *RCAF*

'Kickers' prepare to heave out parachute packed supplies to Fourteenth Army from a Canadian Dakota somewhere over Burma. *RCAF*

An Elephant Squadron crew climb over rice bags to their positions in the Dakota transport. In the foreground is the CO, Wg Cdr R. Gordon DFC. In the background, left to right, Flg Off G. B. Coyle, Flt Off F. V. Cooper, Flt Off C. O. Simpson, and Flt Lt J. W. Dolphin. *RCAF*

This unofficial badge design, seen in Burma with squadron members, was the forerunner of the official badge of the Elephant Squadron, approved in 1946 by Chester Herald. *RCAF*

Below: The official badge of 436 Squadron Royal Canadian Air Force. *RCAF*

traced directly to this change. More than moderately interested in this problem was Air Marshal Sir Keith Park KCB, KBE, MC, DFC, Allied Air Commander-in-Chief South East Asia, who happened to be making an inspection visit at the time. He agreed that the matter should be investigated immediately. Largely due to data accumulated by 436 on the relative merit of the 'T' oil, the original order was reversed and air-craft serviceabilities rose again to normal level.

By this time the aerial supply lines were begin-ning to stretch beyond what was considered to be economical flying distance for the unit. From 10 May for two days, operations were suspended while trunks were packed and moved 70-miles south-east to Kyaukpyu, on Ramree Island. Coincident with the arrival at Ramree, the monsoon, that eminent precipitation producer which as early as 2 May had inundated and rendered temporarily unserviceable several destination airstrips in southern Burma, began to live up to its reputation. Largely for this reason the squadron's haul fell off sharply for two days. Once acclimatised however, they bounced back, and in the last two weeks of May they averaged 161 tons daily. On 20 May and 31 May a total of 20 crews logged the coveted but elusive 'fourth sortie' — this flying of four sorties in a day was a special target aimed at by Combat Cargo Task Force crews. The last day of the month was the squadron's best day of all, 74 sorties being flown and 243 tons airlifted. That day the footsloggers benefited in many ways, not the least of which concerned 13 tons of one bottled comfort and 10 tons of another — without a permit. The monsoon did indirectly cause the loss of one air-craft on the ground — Dakota KG724 — so deeply mired in the mud of Mingaladon that it had to be abandoned, eventually stopping a runaway Spitfire and being reduced to scrap.

By 1 June the USAAF squadrons were depart-ing India and Burma for another theatre of opera-tions. Their withdrawal meant the loss of weather reporting and forecasting facilities sponsored by the USAAF. Though unable to combat the monsoon on the ground, the Elephants assayed to fight in the air by a substitute weather service of their own. So was born 'Watchbird' which was the brain-child of Wg Cdr R. A. Gordon, a simple yet surprisingly effective system of airborne sur-veillance. Usually one crew would get airborne at 04.30hr — an hour before regular take-off time — and watch and report the weather over a designated area until 11.30hr. A relief crew would then take over and report the weather for the rest of the working day.

The Elephants were active in their air supply function for Combat Cargo Task Force until the last day of August 1945, thereby sharing with their co-workers 435 Chinthe Squadron the honour of being the RCAF's last squadron to carry out operations in the World War 2 period. On that day, for the record, they flew seven trips, airlifted 29,400lb and seven passengers. With these flights they bowed out as an operational entity in the South East Asia theatre. How typical was their last entry in the squadron diary for the Burma period: 'Rainfall at base during August has totalled 57.34 inches.' (The British *annual* average is 30in!) In a short but highly intensive eight months in SEAC the Elephants piled up a most impressive set of statistics. Logging some 32,000 hours whilst covering about 4,000,000 miles by air, they airlifted nearly 29,000 tons of food, military necessities, and 'treats and com-forts' among other things, to sustain soldiers and civilians alike. In addition they transported more than 15,000 troops, casualties and passengers. Having no protective armament other than sidearms, they were wide open to enemy ground fire and aerial attack. Moreover, they faced the constant threat of forced landings or bailing out over impenetrable jungle inhabited by wild animals, unpredictable natives, and a merciless enemy. On half their flights they were assailed by their most formidable foe of all, that being, of course, the tropical monsoon. No squadron had better fulfilled its motto more than the Elephants with their *Onus Portamus*. They truly did carry the load, and in some of the most adverse con-ditions imaginable.

Commencing on 25 August 1945 the Ele-phants set course for the UK following the same route as their sister squadron — an 8,000-mile trip of 44hr flying time — to RAF Down Ampney. With many new aircrews the squadron continued its work in Europe until June 1946, when the squadron flew back home to Canada. On 22 June 1946, 436 Squadron was officially disbanded, having contributed a splendid chapter to the history of the Royal Canadian Air Force.

Below: Photo taken at Mawbubyin during April 1945 with Dakota in the background with title 'Canucks Unlimited' on the fuselage. The group, left to right, are Flt Lt R. S. MacCartney; Sqn Ldr F. E. W. Smith; Sqn Ldr R. L. Denison; Air Marshal Sir Keith Park, Allied Air Commander-in-Chief. South East Asia Command; Sqn Ldr J. A. Ferguson and Wg Cdr R. C. Gordon, the CO of 436 Squadron. *RCAF*

In SAAF Service

Lt Peter Norman Smith of the
South African Air Force, who, with his
Dakota crew flew 140 sorties to RAF
Gatow during the Berlin Airlift, stands
in the doorway of a Mk IV transport
coded NU-P-Poppa from 240 OCU
one of the many RAF transports used
on the airlift. *MoD*

Operating under 216 Group RAF, the first South African Air Force Dakota squadron to operate in the Middle East was No 28 with the appropriate motto 'Portamus — We Carry'. The first CO was Maj A. A. D. McKellar and the first entry in the operational record book reads: 'In humble surroundings at SAAF Base Depot Almaza, Cairo, Middle East; 28 Squadron is born'. The date was 1 June 1943. The unit personnel were drafted from Nos 24 and 35 Flights SAAF and by August equipment included five Dakotas, seven Ansons and two Wellington aircraft. A Flight was based at Castel Benito, Tripoli, and B Flight at Ras El Ma, Morocco. By September detachments were based at Pachino, Sicily; Lecce, Italy; Oudja, Morocco, and Setif, Algeria, with a detachment moving to Bari, Italy, during November and one to Rabat, Morocco, in January 1944. By June 1944, all the detachments were withdrawn and the squadron was based at Maison Blanche, Algeria, the Dakotas flying routes covering North Africa, the Western Mediterranean, Italy and France.

By the end of April 1944, 28 Squadron was equipped with 30 Dakotas. A special flight to Paris was flown on 3 September 1944, transporting the French National Committee of Liberation from Algiers in two Dakotas. During 1944 a total of 87,029 passengers and 33,692,361lb of freight were carried and total flying hours for the year amounted to 38,859.

Personnel for a second SAAF Dakota squadron for the Middle East sailed from Durban on 8 February 1944, arriving at Cairo West the following month. On 12 March 1944, No 44 Squadron was activated at Cairo, the aircrew being trained with Dakota crews from Nos 27, 28 and 216 Squadrons RAF. The first operational flight by a 44 Squadron Dakota took place on 14 July 1944, with a trip to Naples, Italy. Detachments operated as required from Khartoum, El Adam, Habbaniyah, Athens and Bari. A regular two-week schedule operated through Habbaniyah down the Persian Gulf, returning along the South Arabian route via Khartoum. Special flights and diplomatic missions were flown to the USSR, St Jean, Castel Benito, Turkey, Bucharest, Belgrade, Albania, Salonika, Marseille, Forli and Zara. In addition the Daks flew passengers and freight plus regular runs with blood plasma to forward base hospitals.

October 1944, found both SAAF Dakota squadrons making new records. Deteriorating weather failed to cause any falling off in the performance of 28 Squadron at Maison Blanche. Early in the month four Dakotas were grounded by weather at Naples, and two at base, whilst six other flights had to be cancelled. Despite this the total flying hours for the month amounted to 3,148 with a total of 29 transports on strength. Further east, 44 Squadron found compensation for poor weather in the Mediterranean, for the monsoon period was now over and conditions were excellent on the flights to the Persian Gulf. October proved to be the busiest month since the squadron was formed, and a total of 1,069 hours were flown on routine flights. In addition, Lt-Col S. P. Jones's crew flew 1,006 hours on special flights, 53 of them at night. This pilot commanded a Dakota based in the USSR during Winston Churchill's conference with Stalin. Aden was added to the list of detachments, and at the end of October four Dakotas were sent to Bari to reinforce 267 Squadron RAF under 249 Wing of the Balkan Air Force.

A Dakota from 28 Squadron had the distinction of saving Gibraltar. It was a popular superstition that if the Barbary apes, which

Right: Whilst on a supply dropping mission in the Balkans to Yugoslav troops, a Dakota transport from 44 Squadron SAAF had the control cable to the rudder rendered useless when a 'one in a thousand' rifle shot by German ground forces cut the cable. The pilot, Lt W. J. Lindsay, managed to control the aircraft whilst his wireless operator, Sgt S. E. Griffith, sent out an SOS. The Dakota was landed safely at an airfield in Yugoslavia. *Official SAAF*

Top left: World War 2 line-up of SAAF Dakotas. The second in line is Mk III 6842 — ex RAF KG766 and ex-C-47A-30-DK 43-48049 c/n 13865. This aircraft went to the Rhodesian AF in 1947 and as R3702 was destroyed in Mozambique by a Stella missile on 31 May 1977, whilst being flown by Flt Lt B. Collocott. *D. Becker*

Centre left: This Dakota Mk IV '6848' GZC from 5 Wing SAAF was in use on the shuttle service during 1945 and was photographed at the South African Air Force base at Pietersburg. The shuttle included the UK on its schedule. This aircraft was still in SAAF service as of June 1981. *D. Becker*

Below: Another SAAF Dakota, '6871' GZDC from 5 Wing. It is ex-RAF ex-FL583 ex-C-47A-1-DK 42-92215 c/n 11991. The aircraft survived World War 2 and is believed to be still flying in South Africa. *D. Becker*

inhabit the Rock — a British fortress since 1713 — ever disappeared, Gibraltar would cease to belong to Britain. During 1944 the ape population reached an all-time low and so, in July, a high priority load of VIP Barbary apes was safely delivered to Gibraltar by Lt L. M. Boshof. During November 28 Squadron lost a Dakota when a USAAF aircraft taxied into it.

The transports of 44 Squadron flew 1,031 hours by day and 63 hours by night on special tasks, as against a mere 535 by day and 46 by night on scheduled and routine duties. Taking into account air tests and other flying, the squadron monthly total for November was barely 1,730 hours, as against an estimated capability of 3,300 hours. Three Dakotas were taken over from 267 Squadron RAF on 2 December to fly for Mediterranean Air Transport Services on the route covering Casablanca, Gibraltar, Oran and Algiers under the control of 284 Wing.

By February 1945, 44 Squadron had moved its HQ to Bari, Italy and operated under 249 Wing. Supplies were regularly dropped to partisans in Yugoslavia and partisan troops were flown into Belgrade, with Allied PoWs and wounded partisans brought out on return. Quite often landings were made on specially prepared airstrips in or very near enemy occupied territory. During March 1945 the squadron evacuated its 1,000th Yugoslavian partisan casualty, and all in all over 1,200 partisans were evacuated.

The above operational and other sorties earned high praise from senior RAF personnel, and the following is the text of one message of congratulations:

'From OC 151 Wing RAF — dated January 1945.
During their stay in the Persian Gulf, there has been a record spell of bad weather in the district, and airfields at Bahrein and Sharjah have been unserviceable more often than not, but in spite of all difficulties, the aircrew have kept the Gulf service going. Thanks to them, all our staging posts received their extra supplies, although the airfields were officially unfit for any other aircraft to land, and there was some doubt as to whether they would be able to take off again after delivering Christmas freight.'

Daylight supply drops over Yugoslavia continued up to 5 May 1945, and 44 Squadron fulfilled its commitments with 24 Dakotas, as six had been withdrawn. Ten of the unit's Daks were occupied on special operations up to 9 May, two were detained in Bucharest for six days, three were in the United Kingdom, and two others were unserviceable. With the Balkan Air Force, the surrender in Italy had no effect on operations. The squadron received from the AOC Balkan Air Force the following message. 'I have received the following signal from RAF Landing Ground Party at Piccadilly Hope, Yugoslavia', the signal read. 'Partisan HQ wish to join my party in congratulating and thanking 44 Squadron SAAF on their feat in evacuating their thousandth body from landing ground. I would like to add the congratulations of all of us at this HQ on this fine job by your squadron.'

It was then revealed that the landing strip in Yugoslavia had been occupied by the enemy for 24 hours between 22 and 23 March. Lt Lindsay had his rudder cable shot away by flak on 18 March, but landed his Dakota safely at Zara. The squadron felt more than satisfied at being able to make a really tangible contribution to the war effort, even though delays in getting clearance from the Russians in Bucharest caused annoyance and irritation. On 241 round trips flown during March, 109 were on support operations and 49 on special flights.

In the 19 months in which 44 Squadron operated in the operational theatre, they flew a total of 39,423 hours, which averaged out at over 2,000 hours per month. The wartime role of the squadron came to an end on 6 December 1945, when it was disbanded at Bari, Italy, and personnel were repatriated back home to the Union.

Earlier 28 Squadron had commenced its homeward trek during September, all personnel being transported in the unit's Dakotas. However it was still kept active taking an integral part in the 'Shuttle Service' from Cairo to Pretoria during the latter half of 1945 and early 1946. Two contingents were later to participate in the Berlin Airlift.

Below: As soon as a landing strip was cleared near the battle front the Dakotas flew in with supplies and flew the wounded out. Photo shows the scene at a typical landing strip near Taranto, Italy on 7 September 1943, showing bombs being unloaded from a Dakota for possible use by the RAF Curtiss P-40 Tomahawk fighter-bombers parked in the background. *IWM*

By August 1960 some 11,500 troops from nine nations were on duty with the UN Force in the Republic of the Congo helping to restore order and calm in the country. This UN Dakota has arrived from Leopoldville at Luiabourg, provincial capital of Kasai. Tunisian troops are seen unloading the Dakota ONU 206. *UN*

Postwar Operations

The Berlin Airlift

The Berlin Airlift began in June 1948. It was started to defeat the blockade which had been gradually imposed by the USSR upon the three Western sectors of the city. For political purposes, the Russians had suspended all traffic by road, rail and inland waterway between Berlin and the Western Zone of Germany, which was controlled by France, the United Kingdom and the USA.

On 26 June 1948, a total of 32 Douglas C-47 flights from Wiesbaden AFB to Templehof brought 80 tons of vitally needed supplies to the now besieged city. When the airlift began there were less than 100 C-47s based in USAFE. On that same date the RAF also began to support the aircraft from bases in the British Zone of Germany. Six Dakotas, airborne under an Operation Order known as 'Knicker' provided the pattern upon which the most colossal air operation in history was built. They flew from Wunstorf to Gatow, the first Dak to land being from 18 Squadron carrying 6,000lb of food. Within three weeks Operation 'Vittles', the US code-name for the airlift, was growing with 54 C-54 Skymasters and 105 'Gooney Birds' or C-47s carrying the load of the US effort. On 1 October 1948, the USAF retired the C-47 from the airlift in favour of the larger C-54 Skymaster.

There were many incidents and quite a few accidents. A Dakota at Wunstorf was loaded in error with the load destined for an Avro York — the Dakota load was normally 5,500lb and York's 11,500lb. As soon as the overloaded Dak commenced its take-off run it was apparent all was not well, but it eventually crawled into the air. When the loading error was discovered, the pilot was requested to return, but apparently having got off the ground he was determined to deliver the extra load to Berlin.

Many civil contractors were called upon to assist with the refurbishing of stored Dakotas and

Below: The first RAF aircraft to land at Gatow during the airlift was a Dakota from 18 Squadron with B. G. Hughes (Pilot), S. A. Botsford (Navigator) and K. Driffill (Signaller) as crew. The inscription on the Dakota reads: 'This was the first aircraft and first crew to fly on Operation "Plainfare". Landed Gatow 0400hrs 26 June 1948. Total sorties by Dakotas in 12 months 2,773. *RAF Museum*

Above: Loading and refuelling RAF Dakotas lined up on the airfield at Lübeck during the airlift. The wartime invented PSP is still proving its usefulness. Second aircraft in line is Dakota KK198 'N for Nuts', ex-C-47-B-20-DK 43-49714 c/n 15530. *RAAF*

Right: On display in the Officer's Mess at RAF Gatow, which borders on the Russian Zone of Berlin, hangs this plaque which is a fitting tribute to the many RAF and Commonwealth crews plus the ubiquitous Dakota transport which operated from the RAF bases at Wunstorf, Fassberg and Lübeck, flying vital supplies along the corridors into Berlin. *RAF Gatow*

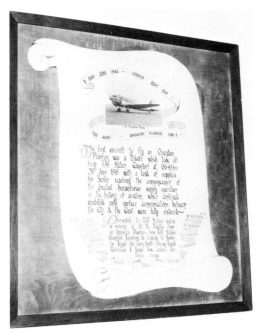

Above left: Night scene at RAF Honington, Suffolk, as a 'Plumber Flight' Dakota is unloaded with tyres plus an engine for a Avro York transport. Aircraft is 'G-George', KN274, ex-C-47B-20-DK 43-49948 c/n 15764. *MoD*

Above: Both passengers and freight were carried on the flights out of Berlin with RAF Dakotas including the elderly and young children, seen here on arrival at an airfield somewhere in the British Zone of Germany. This was the greatest mercy airlift ever known. *RCT Museum*

Left: On 26 June 1948, C-47 Skytrains of the USAF in Europe commenced flights from Wiesbaden air base to Templehof carrying supplies for the besieged city of Berlin. This was a daily scene at Templehof in the early days of the huge airlift operation. Later Douglas C-54 Skymasters took over from the smaller C-47 Skytrain transport aircraft. *USAF*

Centre left: The airlift into Berlin was the largest peacetime operation ever undertaken in terms of aircraft movements and tonnage flown. Depicted is a USAF Skytrain being marshalled to its unloading point at Templehof, Berlin, at night. Most of the USAF C-47s came from the European Air Transport Service (EATS). *USAF*

Bottom left: The personnel from the 86th Tactical Fighter Wing based at Neubiberg air base during the period of the airlift, decided they would ensure the children of Berlin would not be without toys at Christmas. This Douglas C-47A-20-DK, 42-93087 c/n 12960 from the 86th Air Base Group, was used to carry the gifts into Berlin and was appropriately marked. It was intended to include a young camel, but it died. *Merle Olmsted*

the overhaul of those operating on the airlift. Scottish Aviation overhauled a total of 71 Daks between August 1948 and May 1949, all for airlift use. Airwork Limited, Field Aircraft Services and Marshalls of Cambridge were all involved with either the Daks themselves or overhaul of the Pratt & Whitney Twin Wasp engines. RAF Honington, Suffolk, was the home of the 'Plumber Flight' with six Daks which each month flew some 60,000 miles carrying between 400 and 500 tons of spares to airlift bases in Germany. Transports on the airlift had a much higher landing rate so the strain on tyres, brakes and undercarriages increased. Honington served as a clearing house for all individual spares required by airlift aircraft.

British European Airways in Germany received plans for augmenting the military Operation 'Plain Fare' on 1 August 1948, the first civil aircraft arriving three days later. The civil airlift started in earnest on 5 August the fleet at that time including nine Dakotas from Air Contractors, Air Transport (Jersey), Westminster Airways, Kearsley Airways, Scottish Aviation, and Trent Valley Aviation. By 21 September the civil fleet had doubled in size. Ciro Aviation and British Nederlands contributed more Daks and this month saw the completion of the first 1,000 sorties. By November the Dakota participation in the civil airlift was 17 aircraft, but as contracts expired the Dak was withdrawn in favour of the four-engined Halton transport aircraft. BOAC provided three Daks on the airlift for just over a month during 1948.

It was May 1949 before the Russians eventually reopened the surface routes into Berlin. So ended the greatest humanitarian supply operation in the history of aviation, in which the Dakota played a major role.

Top: Air Contractors with three Dakotas including G-AIWD, were one of the first airlines to assist on the airlift from RAF Fassberg during 1948. G-AIWD was ex-KG658 ex-C-47A-25-DK 42-93551 c/n 13475 and flew 53 sorties to Berlin for a total of 154 flying hours. *Author's collection*

Above: During World War 2 BOAC operated nearly 60 Dakotas initially in full RAF livery the crews holding temporary RAF rank. They used three Dakotas on the airlift for a period of just over a month, during which time G-AGNG flew 33 sorties in just over 89 hours flying time. It is ex-KK216 'OFZB', ex-C47B-20-DK 43-49736 c/n 15552. *BOAC*

Right: Trent Valley Aviation Limited of Nottingham contributed a single Dakota, G-AJPF, to the airlift which accomplished 186 sorties in just over three months and accumulated 504 flying hours. It was ex-KG644 ex-C-47A-25-DK 42-93534 c/n 13456. *Author's collection*

106

Malaysia - Operation Firedog

On 27 June 1948, the Civil Government of the Federation of Malaya declared a State of Emergency. A number of isolated bands of jungle irregulars, who had fought a small and rarely successful campaign against the occupying Japanese Army during World War 2, had been taken over and banded together by a few key Chinese and Malayan Communists almost before the war was over. They formed a small but potentially dangerous, unseen and almost unknown army the aim of which was to gain control of Malaya and Singapore using the classic formula laid down by Mao Tse Tung. By the spring of 1948 the Malayan Communist Party had failed to gain power through economic and industrial subversion and the Malayan People's Anti-British Army — later renamed the Malayan Race's Liberation Army — was formed. By attempting to fan the flames of anti-British feeling and recruiting by terrorism the party entered the protracted war phase of the Mao method. What had begun as a spot of local trouble had become the forerunner of modern guerrilla warfare. The mountainous jungle covered country of the Malaya Peninsula was eminently suitable to the principle of Mao's Master Plan, hiding the enemy and hindering the Federal and Allied troops. It was against this background that the Malayan Emergency began.

With the outbreak of hostilities against the Communists, 48 Squadron, together with 52 and 110 Squadrons, all equipped with Dakotas, evolved a technique of supply dropping in the mountainous jungles which enabled them to drop supplies to troops and police all the year round. Numerous bases and forts deep in the mountains came to depend entirely on air supply for their existence. This demanding flying over difficult terrain in swiftly changing monsoon weather took its toll, and up to 1957 four transports with all their crews were lost in operations over Malaya.

By 1952, the security forces were getting on top of the guerrillas. For propaganda purposes, the first 'sky-shouting' with loud-hailers was undertaken during November 1952 by Austers, and later by Dakotas. This war was won by land forces marginally aided by air power and ended by political means. As demands for 'Voice' aircraft increased it was decided to form a 'Voice Aircraft Flight' which became C Flight of 267 Squadron, based at Kuala Lumpar. The Flight was established with three Dakotas — KP277 *Faith*, KJ955 *Hope*, KJ810 *Charity*, and two Taylorcraft Auster aircraft. The first RAF

Below left: Sgt H. W. Batty BEM at his control station as 'Tannoy Operator' during 'Voice' operations from a Dakota in Malaya during Operation 'Firedog'. *MoD*

Bottom left: Interior of the 'Voice Flight' Dakota looking forward, which indicates the amount of equipment carried in both KP277 and KJ955, both used extensively and with great success in Malaya. *MoD*

Below: Seen over the dense jungle of Malaya is Dakota Mk IV KP277 (ex-C-47B-40-DK 44-77247 c/n 16831) with its four speakers slung under the fuselage. It carried the name *Faith*. *J. Merryshaw*

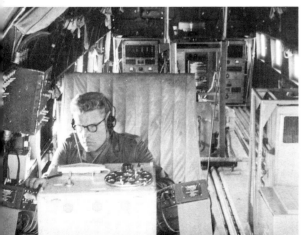

Above: Also used in Malaya during Operation 'Firedog' until July 1960, were Dakotas from the RNZAF. Depicted is NZ3546 from 42 Squadron ex-C-47B-35-DK 44-76981 c/n 16565. *RNZAF*

Right: The RNZAF and RAAF assisted the RAF in Operation 'Firedog' in Malaya. Photo shows Dakota NZ3552 (ex-C-47B-45-DK 45-959 c/n 34222) from 41 Squadron on a supply drop over the Malayan jungle during July 1950. *RNZAF*

Below right: RNZAF Dakota NZ3546 (ex-C-47B-35-DK 44-76981 c/n 33313) being parked on the PSP parking area at Kuala Lumpur during October 1949. This Dakota was one of the last to serve with the RNZAF into the 1970s. *RNZAF*

Bottom right: The last Dakota sortie flown from the RAAF base located at Butterworth, Malaya was on 10 December 1968, to a Police field force fort along the border of Thailand and West Malaysia. The Dakota was one of six from the RAAF based at Butterworth, and carried four Royal Corps of Transport despatchers. *RAAF*

Dakota arrived on 12 June 1954, and was ready for operations 11 days later; a second Dak arrived on 13 July 1954 and the strength of aircraft was up to establishment by the first day of October 1954.

At one time when eliminations were occurring frequently, the messages from Voice aircraft were known as the 'Stop Press of the Jungle', and although it was almost impossible to credit Voice aircraft with actual numbers of surrendered terrorist personnel, almost all terrorists admitted to having heard the Voice aircraft Dakota at sometime or another, and as proof of the esteem in which the Voice aircraft was held, several surrendered terrorists stated: 'We heard from the Voice aircraft that "X" had been eliminated, so we knew that it must be true.'

Operation 'Firedog' ceased on 31 July 1960.

The Korean War

The first major aerial confrontation after World War 2 came about as a result of the first failure to contain the Cold War and the first test of the United Nations' ability to combat world events. On Sunday 25 June 1950, Communist controlled North Korean forces invaded the US-aided South. As the ill-equipped South Korean army fell back everywhere, the US first evacuated their advisors and their families using Douglas transports based in Japan, including C-47 Skytrains. Some of these were attacked on the ground by aircraft of the small Russian-equipped

North Korean Air Force. On 20 October 1950, 40 C-47 Skytrains and 71 C-119 Boxcars were used in the UN drive into North Korea when US Combat Cargo Command dropped 2,860 paratroops and 300 tons of supplies north of Pyongyang. Douglas C-47s were later used to evacuate the wounded of the US 1st Marine Division — trapped in the Chosin Reservoir area and a total of 4,689 troops were flown out from an airstrip at Hagaru. The Korean war eventually reached a stalemate in May 1953, and on 27 June 1953 an armistice was agreed

Left: The first USAF Douglas C-47 Skytrain to land at Taejon airfield after its capture from Communist forces by the US 24th Infantry Brigade was on 29 September 1950, and was a late model Oklahoma City-built C-47D-45-DK, 45-1007 c/n 17010 coded '29'. *USAF*

Below: On temporary loan from the US 5th Air Force to the Korean Air Force (South), for Presidential use, was this C-47D-1-DK, 43-48301 c/n 14117, seen parked at K-4 Sachon air base during 1951. Note the South Korean markings on the fuselage. *B. C. Reed*

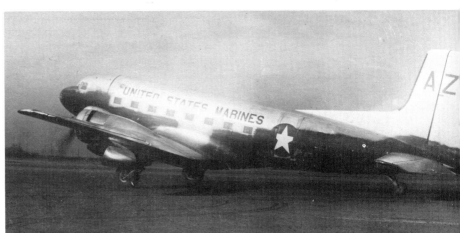

Above: USAF C-47s redesignated RC-47Ds were used as parachute flare droppers to allow Douglas B-26 Invader light bombers to attack the Chinese by night as they drove south in Korea. Photo shows the interior of a RC-47D with its crew preparing parachute flares for dropping. *B. C. Reed*

Top right: On 26 November 1950, C-47 Skytrains from Flight 13 of the Royal Hellenic Air Force became attached to the USAF 21st Troop Carrier Squadron to assist in Korea. These transports included 92620 *Jupiter*, 92622 *Neptune* and 92630 *Mars*. *C. Trask*

Above right: Rare photo depicting a Douglas R4D-8 BuNo 50782 'AZ' c/n 43366 with a hastily finished black anti-glare underside for use on night intruder operations with parachute flares. Photo taken at K-16 air strip, Seoul, South Korea, after the end of the armistice. *C. N. Trask*

Far right, top: Dakota A65-86 (ex-C-47B-30-DK 44-76547 c/n 16131) from No 86 Transport Wing RAAF based in Japan, flying near the rebuilt city of Hiroshima during the Korean conflict. RAAF Dakotas flew a scheduled service to their personnel fighting in Korea, from Japan and Australia. *RAAF*

Right: Throughout the conflict in Korea the Korean National Airlines offered a limited service to and from Japan. This Douglas DC-3A is seen taxying at Tokio Airport, Japan, and is registered HL-06. *C. N. Trask*

110

UN operations

This association of nations, pledged to maintain international peace and security, was inaugurated during the closing stages of World War 2 when the delegations of no less than 50 nations signed the Charter of the United Nations on 26 June 1945. The membership today is well over a hundred. Under the direction of the Security Council, one of the main organs of the UN, military forces may be deployed to restore order, or bring succour, to troubled areas. On numerous occasions aircraft ranging from light liaison types to heavy transports, plus helicopters, have been supplied by member nations to work directly under UN control.

The first occasion for the use of UN forces was during the early postwar disputes between Arab and Jew as the United Kingdom withdrew from her unhappy burden of the Palestinian mandate. During this conflict a small number of RAF Dakotas were amongst the aircraft destroyed.

Since that time numerous aircraft types, including the Dakota, have been used by the UN forces and after the UN flag was officially adopted by the General Assembly on 20 October 1947, it was policy to carry the flag, in full colour of blue and white, as a fin or fuselage marking. The standard finish for UN aircraft was white overall, the traditional neutral colour, with cheat lines of light blue. However, livery did vary for different types and for different theatres of operations. The white ex-RCAF DHC-3 Otters and C-47 Dakotas despatched to the Congo had UNITED

Right: United Nations Dakota 75640 seen at the Gaza Strip in Egypt during 1954. It flew in supplies and personnel three times a week and was the only UN link with the outside world, except for the long trans-desert train journey to the Nile Valley. *UN*

Far right, top: Aircraft used by Lt-Gen E. L. M. Burns, Commander UN Emergency Force in the Gaza Strip from 1956 to December 1959. Aircraft is ex-USAF VC-47D-10-DK 43-49079 c/n 14895 used by the United States Air Force in Europe. *N. C. Parker*

Far right, centre: Fresh troops from Sweden arrive at El Arish airfield to replace time expired Swedish troops after serving with the UN Emergency Force at Gaza. Aircraft are ex-RCAF, one being '989' ex-C-47B-35-DK 44-77134 c/n 33466. *UN*

Far right, bottom: Supplies are brought in by UN Dakota to the UN Emergency Force post at the Gulf of Aqaba end of the International Frontier during April 1959. The aircraft is '656' ex-RCAF ex-C-47A-40-DL 42-23970 c/n 9832. *UN*

NATIONS in 18-inch letters on the starboard side of the fuselage and NATIONS UNIES on the port side.

The Dakota has been a workhorse for the UN since its inception and has served with UN forces and missions in Indonesia, Greece, Palestine, India, Pakistan, Gaza strip and Sinai, Congo, Lebanon and Korea. All of these missions have used at least one Dakota transport. The Congo mission had 10 in service at one time. In all cases the aircraft were used for carrying passengers and freight, plus ambulance and observation duties. The RCAF, USAF, Italian Air Force and other countries have provided the aircraft and crews to the UN for use by the missions.

During the 1950s No 115 Air Transport Unit — an RCAF unit with the UN — was based at El Arish, Egypt. On 17 June 1958, Dakota Mk 4 KN666 from this unit was forced by United Arab Republic MiG-15 jets to land at Abu Suer, allegedly for not flying the established air corridor.

The veteran Dakota was eventually replaced by the RCAF Caribou because of the latter's versatility, especially in those remote areas where only rough and short landing strips were available.

Vietnam

USAF C-47 Skytrains were involved in South-east Asia as early as 1946, when Viet Minh forces commanded by Gen Vo Nguyen Giap attacked the French. From the summer of 1950 and throughout the next two decades, USAF personnel — military advisors, maintenance and supply experts, combat crews and the like — were ordered into French Indochina and, later, to its successor states South Vietnam, Laos and Cambodia in support of national policy. In January 1953, Philippine-based USAF personnel were sent to Nha Trang air base to help the French maintain C-47 Skytrains loaned for use against the Viet Minh. In 1954, several months before the battle of Dien Bien Phu, several hundred USAF mechanics were provided to help keep US-loaned aircraft, including Douglas C-47s, in flying condition. In September 1954, the USA sponsored the creation of an eight-nation South East Asia Treaty Organisation (SEATO) which threw a mantle of protection over Laos, Cambodia and the free territory under the jurisdiction of the State of Vietnam. It will be many years if ever before the full story of operations in South-east Asia is unfolded, because of the secrecy involved in many of the operations. One Douglas DC-3 — N11890 owned and operated by Continental Air Services and built in 1942 with 26,000 hours

Right: US Marine Corps C-117D, BuNo 50834 c/n 43324 from MAG-11, seen parked at Hong Kong on a R&R (Recreational and Recuperation) visit from its base in South Vietnam. *APN*

Below: Douglas C-117D Super-DC3 BuNo 50780 c/n 43398 damaged after a Viet Cong rocket attack. It was based at Cam Ranh Bay. Another C-117D (BuNo 17124 c/n 43310) was damaged during November 1969, when a Viet Cong rocket exploded nearby wounding some of the crew. *US Navy*

Left: A camouflaged South Vietnamese Air Force C-47B-20-DK, 43-49783 c/n 15599, landing at a remote airstrip in the South Vietnam highlands. After the withdrawal of US forces from Vietnam C-47 transport aircraft, plus gunships, were included in the many aircraft left behind. *APN*

Below left: Laotian Army C-47A-90-DL 43-15666 c/n 20132 with the ubiquitous PSP in the foreground. The French were responsible for supplying Laos with their first 10 C-47 Skytrains and for training the crews. Other C-47s were supplied from USAF stocks.
Author's collection

115

flown — broke all records on 23 March 1975, when it evacuated 98 refugees, all orphans, plus five attendants, from the Central Highland town of Du Lat and flew them to Saigon. In addition to the record 103 passengers the DC-3 carried a crew of three: pilot Fred B. Walker, co-pilot Edwin Keppler Vaile and a Vietnamese steward. The previous record for the number of passengers carried by a DC-3 was established in 1949, when 84 refugees were evacuated during the fall of China to the Communists.

Above: Seen in landing configuration is Royal Thai Air Force C-47B-45-DK 45-1021 c/n 17024. The Royal Thai Army and Police used the Douglas C-47 with quite a large quantity in service. With the take-over of Communist forces in South-east Asia many C-47s must have been abandoned or captured. *Author's collection*

Right: Cambodian Air Force C-47B-45-DK 45-918 c/n 16921 shares a ramp with a USAF Skytrain and other commercial transports somewhere in South-east Asia. The Skytrain was often the only suitable aircraft for flying into remote airstrips located in equally remote territory, often located within earshot of the Viet Cong. *Author's collection*

Centre right: Although carrying registration marks used by Formosa, this Douglas DC-3 B879 carried Air America as its owner and operator. Many clandestine operations were carried out during the Vietnam conflict and very few details of either the operations or aircraft used by Air America appear to be available. B879 appears to be a standard DC-3 converted from a C-47 Skytrain. *APN*

Bottom right: Unusual DC-3 F-VNAH of Hong Viet Nam airlines. Ex-C-47A-90-DL 43-15835 c/n 20301 the aircraft was registered in the days when France had control of the territory. According to the records it is one of 700-odd USAF C-47s supplied to the USSR during World War 2 under Lend-Lease argreement. *J. A. Bagley*

Top left: Daily scene at Tan Son Nhut Air Base in South Vietnam during 1965, showing a parked AC-47 Dragonship, 44-76534 ex-TC-47B-30-DK c/n 16118, void of unit markings. It is possibly from the 4th Air Commando Squadron (Fire Support) who arrived in the Republic of Vietnam on 26 November 1965. *USAF*

Centre left: A USAF crewman stands in the doorway of AC-47 Dragonship 43-48499 (ex-C-47B-1-DK c/n 14315) from the 1st Special Operations Squadron. Spooky operations were usually carried out at night. *Douglas*

Below left: At a rate of 6,000 round per minute, an AC-47 Dragonship fires its three General Electric 7.62mm miniguns at night over enemy occupied Vietnamese territory. *USAF*

Below: An AC-47 flight crew loading Mk 24 flares. On the command of the pilot the crew dropped the flares overboard. Each flare had a 24-million candlepower capability. *USAF*

Above: Dragonship missions were often supported by Douglas EC-47N/P/Q transports with their electronic jamming capabilities. Depicted is '947' from the 363rd TEW Squadron. In order to generate sufficient power for the increased electronics carried in the EC-47Q this model was re-engined with Pratt & Whitney R-2000-7 power plants. *Douglas*

Right: This Douglas HC-47A-1-DK 42-92111 c/n 11875 was the unit 'hack' for the 12th Tactical Fighter Wing equipped with the McDonnell Douglas F-4C Phantom, and based at Phu Cat Air Base, South Vietnam. Photo taken on 20 September 1970. *N. Taylor*

Below right: Close-up of the three General Electric GAU-2B/A 7.62mm miniguns on AC-47 44-76722 'EN' *Spooky* (ex-C-47B-30-DK c/n 16306) from the 1st Special Operations Squadron, 14th Special Operations Wing, based at Pleiku Air Base during December 1967. *R. C. Mikesh*

Old Dakotas Never Die

No review or study of the world's military air arms fails to reveal the presence of that stalwart workhorse, the Dakota. Due to celebrate its Golden Anniversary on 17 December 1985, it is more than a personal tribute to the Douglas C-47 'Dakota', 'Ole Bucketseats', 'Gooney Bird' or just plain DC-3, that today more than an average percentage of the many built are still in service. In addition to the many civil models flying the backdoor airways connecting commuters with the main-line jet routes, some 56 military air arms still use the Dakota as a transport aircraft. This proves, beyond any doubt, that despite numerous attempts by many aerospace manufacturers since World War 2, that there has been no successful replacement. We hope this pictorial review will substantiate that statement. Alphabetically the countries range from Angola to Zimbabwe, and geographically cover every major continent of the globe. As a lasting tribute to this ubiquitous aircraft, there are numerous aircraft on static show in museums, at airports, as restaurants, in storage for possible resusitation, in many parts of the world, all of which goes to show that 'she was the greatest'.

USA: The Douglas Super DC-3 is still in service today with the US Arctic Research Laboratory located at Point Barrow, Alaska, whilst ex-military models are being used by commercial operators. Until recently the type was in service with both US Navy and US Marine Corps units based in the Far East. These are now retired to the 'boneyard' located at Davis Monthan Air Force Base, Tucson, Arizona. The fuel was extracted and a special oil-based mixture was injected to ensure that all working parts are well preserved. All openings are sealed shut with a liquid plastic poured over the entire aircraft to inhibit corrosion. The final resting place is in 2,000 acres of desert along with approximately 4,000 other aircraft awaiting the recall to active duty. C-117D 'Super DC-3' (BuNo 39109 c/n 43313) is seen in line with others of its type at Davis Monthan.   *N. Williams*

Right, top to bottom:

Argentina: For some years Argentina has had an interest in Antarctica, and today 1 Escadrille Antarctico is equipped with a fleet of transport aircraft and helicopters including one LC-47 equipped with skis as depicted. *W. Steeneck*

Cameroun: Since achieving independence in 1960, the ex-French colony of Cameroun has received economic and military aid from France. The transport arm of L'Armée de l'Air du Cameroun is equipped with a variety of transport aircraft including four Douglas C-47s. Depicted is 11705 ex-C-53DO 42-68778 c/n 11705. *Author's collection*

Chad: The small air arm operated by Chad has received assistance from France for some years, but civil war and technical problems have reduced the inventory to a few light aircraft plus nine Douglas C-47 transports. Civil war broke out in March 1980, following a ceasefire agreed between the Chad Government and the National Liberation front in 1979. Depicted is C-47B-15-DK 43-49594 c/n 15410 ex-French Air Force. *APN*

Colombia: The transport element of the Fuerza Aerea Colombiana comprises the military airline Satena, which operates services linking the capital Bagota with distant points around Colombia. The fleet includes Douglas DC-3s, whilst the military element has a fleet of six C-47 Dakotas. FAC-1126 was seen at San Andrés Island, Colombia on 29 June 1980.

Below: *Congó:* Receiving its independance in 1960 the ex-French colony of Congo has a small air arm which includes three C-47s supplied by the French. The year after independence UN forces were called in and the photo was taken during December 1961, and depicts a Katanga Air Force Fouga Magister jet with DC-3s parked on the airstrip. *United Nations*

Above: *Ethiopia:* The war in the Ogaden during 1977-78 introduced Soviet arms and advisors plus Cuban technicians to Ethiopia. The Douglas C-47 was introduced to the Imperial Ethiopian Air Force inventory shortly after World War 2, and today a dozen are included in the assorted transport fleet. The photo depicts a wrecked Ethiopian Airline Dakota ET-AAP (ex-C-47A-25-DK 42-93286 c/n 13181) which became involved in the conflict. *The Daily Telegraph*

Left, top to bottom:

Finland: Under the terms of the 1947 Treaty of Paris, the Finnish Air Force is limited to a strength of 60 combat aircraft and 3,000 personnel. Having operated the DC-2 and DC-3 in a military role, today the transport squadron has seven C-47s in storage for which a replacement is being sought. Depicted is DO-9 C-53D-DO ex-42-68823 c/n 11750. *P. J. Bish*

France: The French Aeronavale continues to operate the Douglas C-47, principally for training by Escadrille 56/S based at Nimes Garons with 20 Dakotas. These will be retired as the Nord 262 replacement arrives, but the last 10 C-47s are forecast to stay in service until 1984. Seen during 1980 are '36' C-47A-35-DL 42-23936 c/n 9798 and '485' C-47B-5-DK 43-48585 c/n 14401. *J. P. Dujardin*

Denmark: During September 1953, a Douglas C-47 transport flight was formed with Eskadrille 721 at Vaerlose with the Danish Air Force, initially equipped with two ex-Scandinavian Airlines DC-3s. Three years later the squadron was strengthened with the addition of six Royal Norwegian Air Force C-47s but the type is now very gracefully being retired. K-685 is C-47A-30-DK 43-48247 c/n 14063 used for paradropping with tape over the protrusions on the cargo door for safety. *RDAF*

121

Above: *Guatemala:* During World 2 the USA granted cash credits to Guatemala under the Lease Lend Act for the purchase of defence materials, including aircraft and equipment, in return for facilities to build defence bases. During 1945 a USAF military mission reorganised the country's air arm which now includes a C-47 transport squadron operating nine aircraft. FAG-560 was photographed on 29 June 1980, at Tikal airfield, Guatemala.

Right, top to bottom:

Honduras: After becoming a signatory to the Rio Pact of 1947, Honduras received a small number of operational aircraft from the USA. These were supplemented by C-47s of which five remain in service. Depicted is FAH-309 in camouflaged livery. *APN*

India: In July 1947 the sub-continent of India was divided into the Dominions of India and Pakistan. India was allocated seven fighter squadrons and one transport squadron from the former RIAF, the latter being equipped with C-47s. In January 1950, India became a republic within the British Commonwealth, and the Royal prefix to the air arm was dropped. In 1951 the IAF had a hard-worked force of some 70 Dakotas of which 25 remain in service today. Camouflaged IJ239 is shown. *R. Riding*

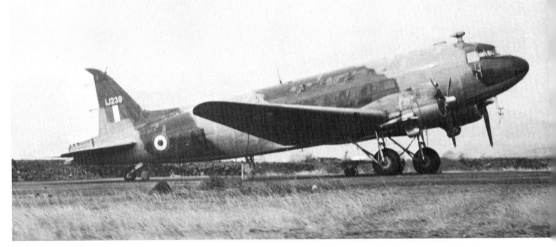

Indonesia: Dutch transfer of sovereignty to the United States of Indonesia took placed on 27 December 1949, after which the Indonesian Air Force (Angkatan Udara Repuplik Indonesia) expanded and re-equipped with the assistance of a Netherlands military mission. On 27 June 1950, the Netherlands East Indies Air Force was disbanded, and all aircraft — including C-47s were handed over to the AURI. A C-47 transport T-480 from the AURI is depicted. *APN*

Left: *Israel:* Constant hostility with neighbouring Arab states, which refuse to recognise its existence, has forced the Republic of Israel to establish and maintain as large and as effective air arm as the country's resources will allow. The Israeli Defence Force is reputed to be the most competent and efficient of all the air arms in the Middle East. Since 1947 Douglas C-47s has been used in many conflicts and several have been converted into rudimentary bombers by the addition of external racks. Today the Israeli Defence Force operates 18 C-47s in the transport and training role, and '09' is depicted.
C. W. Cain

Above left: *Kampuchea:* The kingdom of Cambodia, now Kampuchea, is one of three states which now occupy the area previously known as French Indochina. Independence was granted within the French Union in 1949 and full independence in 1955. A number of ex-French and USAF C-47s were included with the small air arm formed under the title of Royal Khmer Aviation which ceased to exist in February 1979, following the North Vietnam invasion a month before, and it must be assumed that any captured equipment has been integrated with that acquired when South Vietnam fell. This Douglas C-47A-90-DL, 43-15666 c/n 20132, is ex-French Air Force which served on operations in Indochina during the 1950s.
C. P. Russell-Smith

Above: *Libya:* The Libyan Arab Republic Air Force currently operates nine C-47s which are based at Benghazi. C-47B-10-DK 43-49217 c/n 15033 was seen at Luqa, Malta on 25 October 1968. *C. P. Russell-Smith*

Centre left: *Niger:* Formerly part of French West Africa, Niger still receives some aid from France, but has obtained aircraft from West Germany. Its air arm — Force Aerienne du Niger — currently operates a variety of liaison and transport aircraft including two C-47s. This C-47B-10-DK, 43-48990 c/n 14806, is ex-RAF KJ959, ex-French and Mauritania Air Force, and was photographed at Dakar.
APN

Bottom left: *Panama:* The Fuerza Aerea Panamena, first formed in 1969 with assistance from the USA, has no combat aircraft and operates mainly in the transport role for liaison, coastguard and policing duties. This includes surveillance of the Panama Canal, control of which the USA relinquished in 1979. The current FAP inventory includes four Douglas C-47s and photo shows FAP-203 ex-C-47A-90-DL 43-15970 c/n 20436.
Author's collection

123

Right, top to bottom:

Philippines: The Philippine Republic was inaugurated on 4 July, 1946, and the Philippine Air Force became effective three years later. Its first action was against the rebel Hurbalahaps, and for these operations North American Mustang fighter-bombers and Douglas C-47s were employed. Assistance was received from the USA, which included a 99-year mutual defence treaty which was signed in 1951. The fleet of C-47 and AC-47 aircraft is being reduced in numbers. This Douglas C-47B-25-DK 44-76432 c/n 16016 is ex-RAF KN389. *Author's collection*

Sweden: The Douglas C-47 has served with the Swedish Air Force or Flygvapnet as the Tp79 since 1949, and is still in service today with F7 Wing at Satenas who operate seven. The first C-47 — c/n 9103 ex 42-32877 serial 79001 — was based with F8 Wing at Barkaby and on 13 June 1952, took off from Bromma for a radio test flight east of the island of Gotland. It was last heard of on its way back to Bromma and it is thought 79001 was shot down by Russian MiG-15 fighters, as a Catalina (47002) was shot down three days later whilst searching for the missing aircraft. Depicted is 97008 C-47B-30-DK 44-76821 c/n 16405, ex-RAF KN547 and purchased from the West German Air Force in 1975. It still retains its NATO camouflage. *Lars Olausson*

Taiwan: The USA commenced supplying the Chinese government in Formosa with military aid in May 1951, under the supervision of the Mutual Assistance Advisory Group (MAAG). Today the Chinese Nationalist Air Force in Taiwan operates 20 Douglas C-47s. This C-47B-1-DL, 43-16349 c/n 20815, was photographed during a visit to Manila. *C. P. Russell-Smith*

Below: *Turkey:* Still used with the VIP Flight and for Army support, the Turk Hava Kurvetieri operates over 40 C-47s some of which were used to drop paratroops in the dispute in Cyprus during 1974. These are based at Etimesgut, Yesikoy, and Erzurum. C-47 ETI.39 was photographed at Eskiehir during July 1971. *C. P. Russell-Smith*

Top left: *Upper Volta:* The Upper Volta Republic received its independence from France in 1960. The Force Aerienne de Haute Volta currently flies a selection of secondline types supplied by France, including two C-47s. Depicted is 34334. *APN*

Centre left: *Uruguay:* Relying largely upon the USA for security, Uruguay became a signatory to the Rio Pact of 1947, and signed a mutual assistance treaty with the USA in June 1953. At least a dozen C-47s still serve with the Fuerza Aerea Uruguaya today and are based at Caza. *Author's collection*

Below: *Yemen (South):* The air force of the South Yemen People's Republic still continues to benefit from Soviet military aid following the cease fire agreed with the north in early 1979. A transport squadron is equipped, mainly with Russian aircraft, but also has a few C-47s on charge. C-47 '201' (pictured' was converted at Southend. *APN*

Bottom: *Yugoslavia:* On 29 November 1945, the Constituent Assembly of Yugoslavia proclaimed the country a Republic. Steps were immediately taken to lay the foundations of a strong air arm. This included Lisunov Li-2s supplied by the USSR. In March 1953 the first US-built aircraft arrived including a number of C-47s. '71219' was photographed at Dubrovnik on 9 July 1976. *P. J. Howard*

Top : *Zaire:* Originally a Belgian colony known as Congo-Kinshasa at the time of independence in 1960, Zaire today has a tactical and long-range transport air arm known as the Force Zerienne Zairoise which includes 10 C-47s based at Kinshase with 191 and 192 Squadrons. 9T-PKK was photographed at Lubumbashi in 1973.
C. P. Russell-Smith

Centre : *Zambia:* Before independence in 1964, Zambia was known as Northern Rhodesia. Initially the Zambian Air Force was assisted by the UK. Today a quite large transport force operates a variety of aircraft including six C-47s based at Lusaka. AF 104 was photographed at Embakasi during April 1967.   *C. P. Russell-Smith*

Below: *Zimbabwe:* Sources and numbers of most aircraft currently in service with the Zimbabwe, formerly Rhodesia, Air Force are difficult to assess. Most are camouflaged and often do not carry the national insignia or serial numbers. Transport tasks are allocated to 3 Squadron which is equipped with at least a dozen C-47s which contributed to the 'Fire Force' which provided transports for paratroop operations into neighbouring Zambian territory in 'search and destroy' missions. Depicted is a camouflaged 3 Squadron Dakota lacking any identification, with its paratroops resting in the foreground.
Photographers International

Left: The future workhorse of space transportation, the Space Shuttle Orbitor, stands near the great workhorse of civil and military aviation, a DC-3 Dakota, at the NASA flight line at the Dryden Flight Research Center at Edwards AFB, California. Currently NASA operates at least one DC-3 registered N636NA ex-C-47D. *NASA*

Below: This impressive Douglas DC-3 holds the distinction of being the only DC-3 in the world to be mounted on a single, rotating pedestal which allows the aircraft to weathercock into the wind, like a weathervane. It is located at Whitehorse Airport in Yukon and is ex-C-47-DL 41-18540 c/n 4665 which served in India during World War 2 with the US 10th Air Force. A fitting tribute to a Grand 'Ole Lady. *G. Williams*